# Industry Analyst Relations

## - An Extension to PR -

**Ralf Leinemann**

**With Duncan Chapple**

## Contents

ISBN 0-906378-02-8

Published by Folrose Press, PO Box 56354, London SE1 7XZ
www.folrose.com

Printed in the UK
Published simulantously in the United States of America

ISBN 0-906378-02-8
EAN 9780906378021

## List of figures

## Foreword:

## Why industry analyst relations?

In today's world companies in almost all industries depend more and more on a powerful IT infrastructure. Networked computer solutions are no longer just an electronic filing system or an infrastructure for an email system. Today, a company's superior IT infrastructure can become the most dangerous weapon of a company. It allows for quick adaptation to changing business requirements, it enables an agile corporation, it allows fast access to data to support fast decisions, it can become the most powerful sales tool of the company – rather than just supporting a sales organization.

At the same time, an IT infrastructure that is inferior to that of competitors can not only become a bottleneck within the company, but it can even make the company very vulnerable. It can become the Achilles' heel for the company. The company may be unable to respond to competitive moves. It may not be able to adapt to changes in the industry in time or it may simply be in the way of its employees, who spend too much time on infrastructure tasks rather than on activities defined by their job descriptions.

Since an IT infrastructure can be so crucial to the success of a company, the right solution must be selected in a most careful way: A solution must be able to adapt to current and to future business needs; the solution must be supported for quite some time to come; it needs to be flexible; it needs to be expandable. In short: It needs to be a low-risk investment!

The knowledge and skills that are required to make the right decisions is not necessarily available within every company. So, how can CIOs or datacenter managers make the right decision? How can they select the right computer solution, the right network, the appropriate software, the correct services or support? Their staff is not judged able to provide appropriate inputs. The question immediately comes up: is there an opportunity to share best practices with other companies that go through similar decisions (or have done so already) and can already share results?

The need for a sounding board, a knowledge base and an organization that is able to consult in making the right purchase decisions has grown with the increasing impact of high tech infrastructures on the success of companies. Since the status of IT infrastructures has an impact on business decisions that may become crucial to the company the need for help has also gone beyond just consulting in classical IT questions. Decision support may also be needed to make the right outsourcing or off-shoring decisions. Decision support may be needed to identify the appropriate channel to reach the customer. Decision support may be needed to purchase the appropriate production machinery, to align business processes with technical infrastructures, or the other way around – and to allow for business recovery after any kind of disaster.

Industry analysts provide support to help managers find the appropriate answers to all the above questions – and to even more. Industry analysts influence an enormous amount of purchases in the industry. It is estimated to be around half the overall purchases (according to the Kensington Group1 industry analysts influence about 40 to 60 per cent of high-tech spending; according to a survey done by Darwin magazine 55 per cent of CIOs make use of industry analyst market research to make a technology purchase decision). In Western Europe alone it is estimated that they impact business exceeding $100 billion (already in 2000, Duncan Chapple estimated the volume to be more than $125 billion).

In fact, the industry analyst business itself is worth several billion US dollars today.2

On a global basis almost 800 industry analyst firms employ several thousand industry analysts. In Europe alone more than a thousand analysts are counted today.

The majority of these analyst firms, over 500 of them, were established in the USA. Since the 1990's a trend has become more and more visible that these firms open or acquire European and Asia subsidiaries and aspire to become truly global players. One reason for that is certainly the need of the clients – who tend to operate on a worldwide basis – to get a consistent picture across the globe. Analyst firms base their European analysts typically in the Greater London area, one of the two global financial centers. Other European entities are established in Amsterdam, Paris and other major cities.

It is probably fair to say that at, an average, analyst firms established in Europe are more decentralized and significantly smaller than their North American counterparts. Most likely, one reason for that is the different corporate landscape in North America compared to Europe. Language and national boundaries mean that influence, and markets, are more localised. Business in North America is more dominated by major enterprises, while Europe's economy is much more dependent on SMB's (small and medium businesses). Enterprises need analyst services more than, and differently from, smaller companies – and they can afford to pay more. Smaller businesses may not need infrastructures that are as sophisticated as those of worldwide operating corporations, unless they base their business plans on an IT infrastructure that gives them a significant competitive advantage (online banking, online shops, online auctions, etc).

The above makes it obvious that IT vendors who sell mainly to businesses – rather than to consumers – should be interested in industry analysts praising or recommending their products to their clients, i.e. to the vendor's potential customers.

Just as vendors want to reach their customers through a PR program – i.e. via written output from journalists, they want to reach them through an industry analyst program – i.e. via output from industry analysts, both written and oral.

You may ask yourself why a dedicated program is required to address industry analysts. Why can't you address industry analysts simply by incorporating them into

[1] The company ceased to exist end of 2005.

[2] According to a review in March 2001, the magazine Darwin (see e.g. www.drawinmag.com) estimated that industry analysts are paid about $15 billion a year by their clients. Assuming growth rates beyond 10 per cent and the founding of new analyst firms adding to the market size, this value has probably doubled within five years until 2006.

the existing PR program? We will understand later why this is not a good idea at all. You might consider an industry analyst program to be an extension to a PR program, but the two programs are certainly not identical.

While it appears obvious for vendors who focus mainly on B2B[1] business to run an industry analyst program, it can also be a very relevant exercise for vendors who sell mainly to consumers. Consumers would obviously not consult with industry analysts commonly, but they follow recommendations in the media and they listen to experiences their friends have made.

Interestingly enough, journalists and industry analysts are members of a tight network. Reporters tend to double-check news with industry analysts before they write about them. They take advantage of the analysts' knowledge to get a second opinion on industry news and, for the analysts, the cooperation with the press is a welcome way of advertising themselves.

An analyst program is all about becoming a trusted advisor, to use a popular phrase. We will understand later that we actually do not want to influence the influencer, but a good industry analyst program is about building the trusted relations that overcomes the obstacles to informing industry analysts properly. In fact, the influential analysts do not need at all "to be sold to". They will insist on receiving facts. They will not allow their objectivity and independency to be compromised.

But a true industry analyst relations program goes beyond providing information to industry analysts. A true industry analyst relations program consists of several dimensions. It is based on the idea of bringing top industry analysts into a strategic partnership with a company.

Once a true partnership is established, a corporation can benefit in multiple ways from the knowledge that sits with the analysts. In addition to formal services like news flashes or access to research, industry analysts would act as sounding boards. Industry analysts would make themselves available for strategy testing or message testing, either formally billing their time or in return for getting early access to information that helps them in their own planning process.

A successful industry analyst relations program pays a significant dividend on the amount of money put into it.

At the end of this introduction we want to ask the question: why is it that the topic industry analyst relations seems to be a hot button at this point in time. More companies than ever before become interested in adding the function of an analyst relations manager to their portfolio of communication tools. The formation of the Institute of Industry Analyst Relations (IIAR) in the UK and the Deutscher Analyst Relations Arbeitskreis (DARA) in Germany in 2006 confirms the increased interest in the topic.

Several reasons seem to be contributing to this increased interest. An obvious one is that companies more and more understand the influence that industry analysts have on their success in the market. Another reason is that the influential role of industry analysts has indeed grown over time. One could argue that financial analysts needed

1 B2B = business-to-business

support from specialists who are closer to the content. Especially after the collapse of the e-economy voices were needed that were closer to content rather than trying to predict the future only from quarterly earnings announcements. Industry analysts are clearly in the position to bring knowledge together about customer needs, vendor offerings and strategies and markets trends. Thus, vendors more and more realize that they need to be visible to analysts, to be seen as contributors in the industry and ideally to be promoted as current or future industry leaders. A third reason seems to be that more and more local analyst firms are firmly established in Europe and Asia right now. While the number of larger analyst firms tends to consolidate (e.g. Gartner acquiring META or Datamonitor acquiring Ovum), those large firms are not increasing their market share at the same pace. There seems to be a growing demand for smaller and local firms, especially consultancy-led firms that operate on a national level in Europe. Different business needs in Europe or Asia create topics that need to be addressed on a local level (rather than being addressed by headquarters in North America).

# Chapter 1:

## Where do you sell?

In this chapter we want to prepare the foundation for creating a new industry analyst program in our company or organization. We assume we do not work with analysts yet and we will still have to identify the analysts we want to address and include into our program. In order to do so we should understand our own business first. Before we look into some details we do a comparison with public relations, i.e. we do a comparison with our work with journalists.

In public relations we need to ask ourselves some basic questions before we start putting a plan together for PR campaigns. We need to set objectives. We need to segment our customers. We need to define our target media. We need to understand which journalists we want to invite to press conferences. We want to understand how to write a press release so it resonates with the target audience we have in mind. And so on, and so on…

Only after having done some basic analysis of our business and our customers we can go ahead and identify the publications that are read by our targeted customer segment. This planning exercise allows us to maximize the return on the investment we will put into our PR activities.

A simple example shows the value of this approach:

> We assume we sell our products to consumers. We have identified the leading publication in our market covering the product portfolio we address. Let us assume the circulation of that publication is two million. The next biggest publication only addresses six hundred thousand readers. By looking at these numbers it seems to be obvious that we want to focus initially on the larger publication.
>
> Unfortunately, this approach may be incorrect, since we have not looked at two valuable parameters yet. Neither have we looked at the results of the detailed segmentation efforts of our marketing colleagues nor have we looked at the segmentation of the readers addressed by the two publications we have identified.
>
> In our example we may run into the situation that, say, only twenty per cent of the readers of the bigger publication fall into the segment we address with our products. This would be 400,000. The smaller publication, however, is much more focused. It focuses exclusively at readers we address, i.e. consumers we have identified as targets in our marketing segmentation effort. In other words, if we work with the smaller publication, we would reach 600,000 potential customers, or 50 per cent more than in the first case.

The above example shows that we have the option in PR to take a "shot gun" approach, i.e. we spread our resources very widely and do not aim properly, or we dedicate our (typically very limited) resources to quite focused activities – trying to maximize the return on the investment.

The same is true when working with industry analysts. We could attempt to take a shot gun approach reaching out to any analyst we could get hold of. Or we focus on those that are close to our business and – even better – close to our targeted customers.

A shot gun approach with analysts is obviously not recommended at all. It will back fire very quickly. We will not only waste our own valuable time, but we will also waste the time of those analysts that are not really working in our business segment. It is needless to say that they will be annoyed by our calls, emails or visits. If we set their expectation incorrectly, they may even be upset and will feel misguided. This behavior can actually spoil your and your company's reputation very quickly.

Therefore, we want to select the analysts we want to work with very carefully. Every analyst has a well defined competence area, field of interest, focus area or research area. We need to ensure we approach the right analysts addressing the market we compete in, or who at least cover topics that have an overlap with our focus areas.

In order to identify the right analysts we need to understand our own business very well. In the following paragraphs we will bring up a few questions we should ask ourselves (and answer!) before we approach any industry analysts. Many of these questions are very basic. This should not stop us from thinking about them and making ourselves aware of the answers. We will not only need to have the answers for identifying the right analysts for our industry analyst program. We would have to ask the same questions to identify the right analysts or analyst firms to buy research from for our planning department.

In the following, we will address seven questions that should provide some guidance. we should say that in a specific case some of these questions may not be relevant and we may need to replace them by specific questions that are more relevant in the respective industry. But we hope that the questions give a flavor of what we need to consider.

**Do you sell to consumers or to commercial customers?**

Answering this question will have several implications. Your answer may already exclude several analyst firms since they do not address the market you focus on at all. While some address complete markets, some others are only looking after the consumer space or the commercial ("business-to-business") space, respectively. If you are selling industrial solutions in the automotive industry, then you may not want to work with GfK, for example, an analyst firm focusing more on the consumer markets.

The second consequence from answering the above question is to identify the relevant analysts for your business in analyst firms that address the entire market. If you, for example, sell consumer goods, then you may not be interested in talking to a Gartner or an IDC analyst who consults with enterprise customers. But you may be very interested in talking to a Gartner or an IDC analyst who is focused on the consumer market.

A third consequence is based on the way, how these analyst firms influence your customers. While firms that address the commercial market obviously consult with your customers directly, this direct interaction is not happening in the consumer space. However, analysts are very often quoted in the press. Their independent view of the market is a perfect source for journalists. In fact, you will notice after some time that analysts and journalists are networking. They tend to exchange their observations in an informal way very regularly. That has an especially strong influence in consumer markets, where the mass media are most influential.

This third aspect impacts the information we want to share with the analysts. For example, we may want to share customer case studies1 with an analyst in the B2B space. An analyst in the consumer space, however, may be much more interested in how our company addresses the indirect sales channel.

#### What vertical market(s) do you address?

Especially vendors selling in the commercial space tend to segment their customers by vertical markets. Quite a few of the bigger analyst firms tend to employ groups of analysts focusing on vertical markets rather than addressing certain product portfolios. In other words, they would for example address the financial market or the automotive market rather than looking into generic datacenter computing solutions or for example the PC market.

Typically, companies selling in the B2B ("business-to-business") markets need to be prepared to work with both analysts who are more product-focused analysts and those who are more market-focused. They need to be aware that both these groups of analysts would need different types of information, just like a journalist writing for a business publication would need different information compared to a journalist writing for a trade magazine.

#### What type of commercial customer do you sell to?

You may skip this section if your company only sells to consumers. Not all commercial customers are the same. Enterprise customers and small or medium businesses ("SMB") tend to have very different needs. Differences start with the respective lengths of decision cycles. SMBs tend to be more flexible. They make faster decisions and they have different decision criteria. For them cost tends to be a bigger issue than

[1] It should be mentioned in this context that the value of a customer case study or a reference story is perceived differently by different analysts. The majority considers it to be the most important information. Some, however, consider them to be of no value at all. In the first group we should expect to find analysts who consult with vendors rather than with users. In the second group we should expect more those analysts who are in daily contact with users. They should already have a good understanding of customers' implementations and needs. It is of great value to them to see a real life case showing how a similar need was addressed by a specific solution.

for enterprises. They may be satisfied with low-end or mid-range solutions rather than going for top-of-the-line products and services.

Finally, SMBs tend to have a different buying behavior than enterprises. While larger companies are typically looked after by dedicated sales teams, smaller organizations tend to make purchases more like consumers.

When selecting an analyst firm you want to work with, you need to be aware of the type of your customer. Major organizations can easily afford to work with top analyst firms. Smaller companies may not subscribe to their services for two reasons: Their service may be irrelevant to them since it may be far too sophisticated – and it may be too expensive for them.

Often enough smaller analyst firms fill the gap and provide dedicated services for smaller or mid-sized companies. They provide newsletters, consulting services and research notes dedicated to the needs of SMBs, at a price these companies can afford.

So, if we address primarily SMBs we want to ensure that we identify those niche players that service smaller organizations. The usual suspects – the major analyst firms – may not be the best target for our industry analyst program. They may be our prime target, however, if we sell mainly to larger corporations.

### Do you sell direct or through the channel?

Selling direct means that you are in control. You know your customer, you know his needs and you experience market trends first hand. Selling through the channel means reduced understanding of your customers' needs and sometimes even reduced understanding of who your customers actually are. When you sell indirect you have the additional challenge of convincing your channel partners to work with you. You need to offer appropriate margins, you need to offer the right products and marketing support and you need to offer the right long-term strategy. If an independent body like an industry analyst speaks up in your favor this would obviously be a tremendous help for you working with channel partners, regardless, if that is wholesalers, retailers or integration houses.

Several analysts have established a network of channel partners that they poll from time to time to learn about their satisfaction with vendors, their business and trends in the market. It is needless to say that this information can be as valuable as gold for a vendor.

Working with analysts who address the channel, e.g. retailers, has two benefits for a vendor. Firstly, it allows you to influence the channel through analysts that are convinced that you deliver the best solutions and are the best business partner. And secondly, these analysts are a valuable source for information about what is going on in the real world – a world that a vendor may be disconnected from when not interacting with customers directly. And even though in-house market research is done, you would always want to rely on a mix of internal and external research.

Finally, analysts working with the channel are a very good sounding board for market share data. Often enough market share data is based on reports from vendors.

Companies like IDC, for example, provide regular detailed market share data based on information provided by OEMs ("original equipment manufacturers"). Companies like GfK, however, base their numbers on sales numbers from retailers. Comparing both data can reveal quite a lot, like for example it can give you an indication of what is in stock in the channel from which vendor.

**Geographical aspects.**

It is estimated that about 1,000 industry analysts are based in Europe. At least two thirds of those are located in the Greater London area. This does not imply that the UK market is well analyzed while the rest of Europe is not covered appropriately. It only indicates that the majority of the analyst firms have their European headquarters in the UK. Typically, these analysts do not have a UK responsibility, but an international one. They tend to analyze most of the European markets (with a focus on Western Europe, though), often enough including the Middle East and Africa.

Working with these analysts means that you have to be very precise with your communication. If your company is present on an international level, you need to understand that these analysts may be interested in two different kinds of information: They want to understand your international strategies, your business across countries and trends you observe across the region. They also want to understand details from every country including the UK, the country where they happen to be based.

You would have to ensure that the communication with those analysts is not left to your local UK colleagues who may only be able to present a picture of your company in the UK. This may not be the appropriate information to position your company for the entire European region. Your spokespeople need to understand how to position the information they are sharing with analysts.

Several companies have a very good local presence across Europe. IDC, for example has hubs in London and in Prague (for Central and Eastern Europe) and analysts in many countries including Russia, the Middle East and others. Often enough, analyst firms also work with affiliates in smaller countries.

You want to understand these networks before you select the analysts you want to work with. It is obviously a tremendous advantage if an analyst firm has people on the ground in those countries that you are specifically interested in. You may prefer those firms over others who track those countries remotely.

By the way, this statement also holds true on a higher level. Analyst firms that track the European market from outside Europe (i.e. without having any analysts locally in the region) may not be at the top of your list of companies to work with when your business focuses on the European market.

Up to this point, the questions were very basic and it should not have taken us too much time to answer them for our specific business. The following two questions should be considered extensions to the basic set above. Also, they may be considered to be examples for other, similar, questions that may be relevant in specific industries or under special circumstances.

**Decision makers and influencers.**

Working with analysts means that you are interested in impacting customers' buying behavior with the help of third party validation. It also means that you are interested in getting insights in the market. You want to learn about trends, buying behaviors, needs, competitive positioning, etc.

In many businesses, it is crucial not only to understand competitive business results, i.e. sales figures relative to the competition and market share data. It may be more important to understand the dynamics behind the numbers. For example, you want to learn about the state of the market to time your activities correctly. You may need answers to questions like: Is the market still dominated by early adopters or is it maturing and getting ready for what Geoffrey Moore calls "main street"? But, you may also need information on actual customer behavior. For example, both in the consumer world as well as in the commercial space, the person who makes a purchase has not necessarily been the person who drove the purchase in the first place.

The purchase of sweets is often made by a mother, but it was probably initiated or at least strongly influenced by her children. The purchase for a family of certain household goods may be done by a man, but he may only execute the expressed will of a female. In a business environment, the purchase of IT equipment may be done centrally by an IT department, but only after that department consulted with the businesses (or, the other way around, central guidelines demand the departments to buy from a preferred vendor list, which was compiled by the IT department in cooperation with the central purchasing department).

You need to understand what service an analyst company actually provides. Is the company focusing on "number crunching" only, for example by providing regular market share data? Or, are the analysts of that company looking behind the curtain and analyze the market in detail? If they analyze the market in detail, it will be interesting to understand their network, i.e. the source of the information they compile. In a commercial environment, you may ask the question if they work with datacenter managers only, or if they also work with procurement and respective departments being served by the datacenter? Only if they have that complete view they will be able to understand the cause of trends, e.g. understand the motivation of influencers. Only then can they consult you properly.1

In this context it is important to stress the fact that the above is obviously said in the light of becoming the analyst's client, i.e. a purchaser of their research and their consultancy. It must be noted, though, that this information is equally important for your analyst program. If you discover that an analyst does not have the appropriate relation with your customer – those people that make the decision to buy your prod-

[1] A good indication is typically the small print text in analysts' research notes. It explains how information was gathered, e.g. in surveys. In some cases the statistical significance of data can be challenged tremendously. In other cases the information collection process clearly has a strong effect on the result. And in yet other cases it was questionable if the right audience was polled to come to certain statements or conclusions.

ucts or services – then you must question if you want to include this analyst in your program.

It is important to understand, though, that the level of sophistication of an analyst firm is not equal to its influence! And, you must consider whether to integrate analyst firms into your industry analyst relations program that you may not necessarily consult with yourself.

**Initial purchase and aftermarket.**

Many businesses are divided in two parts, the initial purchase of an enabling device and an aftermarket for add-on components or supplies. This includes technical devices and memory solutions (e.g. digital cameras or game consoles or organizers and memory cards, PCs and writable CDs/DVDs), media and ink for printing devices (e.g. printers and cartridges and paper, cash registrars and paper rolls), household items (e.g. coffee machine and filters, vacuum cleaner and dust bins), cars (petrol, oil, regular services), etc.

When selecting an analyst firm to work with you may need to understand if they address the entire market or if they focus on the initial purchase only. When you sell DVD players, you might not be interested in the sales of DVDs, or when you sell ceramic hangers for toilet paper, you may not be interested in the sales of toilet paper itself. But, when you sell vacuum cleaners and fitting dust bins or printers and fitting ink cartridges, then you certainly want to understand the complete picture. This would include interdependencies of initial purchases and the aftermarket.

Some analyst firms address complete markets, some focus on the initial purchase only. Both these firms may come to very different conclusions when analyzing the market and respective trends. They may be equally influential, but articulate very different findings. In your industry analyst work, you may need to address one of these groups specifically and educate them in your direction.

Now that we know the basic questions we should answer them for our business. In order to do so we want to have a closer look into two scenarios. These two scenarios should help you to take the right approach when preparing the grounds for your own industry analyst relations program.

**Scenario 1:**

We assume in this first scenario we want to have a look at a software vendor who is interested to work with industry analysts. In this case we need to understand that there may be two very different drivers for the request.

The first one would be a request for support to decide for the appropriate internal IT infrastructure. The company may need to enhance parts of its computing environment. This would range from identifying the best workstations for their software developers, identifying the best networking solutions to allow for collaborative computing across multiple sites or the best security solutions. It could involve special software solutions providing revision control, network management solutions or others. It could also involve questions around the use of their datacenters, backup strategies or others. Consultancy may also be provided in questions related to the supply chain or outsourcing strategies. To address all the questions, the company would probably identify an appropriate analyst firm very quickly to work with. Companies like Gartner, IDC, Forrester and others should be well prepared to support that software vendor. It is important to note that this approach should not require an analyst relations program, since the software vendor in this example is purely a client of the analyst firm.

The second driver for working with analysts is the software vendor's business itself – selling software solutions. The company should be interested to get second and independent opinions on their strategies and their products. It should be interested in getting an external view on changing customer needs and market trends. In this case the company is looking for an analyst firm that has specialized in software solutions, probably with a focus on the customer segment the vendor is addressing. We assume for a second that our software vendor provides solutions for the oil and gas industry. In that case the vendor is looking for an analyst firm that has a high competency in the utilities sector. Our software vendor would certainly be interested in learning from the research of that analyst firm, but there is also an interest to feed information about its own products and strategies to that analyst firm so it can comment on the company and its products in its research notes and e.g. in press interviews.

The software vendor's business intelligence team will be interested in working with an analyst firm that has a complete view of the market to understand trends that may impact the vendor's positioning or future product developments.

The industry analyst relations team, on the other hand, will focus on working with an analyst firm that has a high impact on customers' buying behavior.

**Scenario 2:**

This second scenario will be significantly more complex.

The second scenario will address the needs of a vendor selling printing devices. Let us assume the company offers a broad range of printers addressing a range of customer segments, from consumer across commercial to industrial environments. Home photo printers are offered to consumers, commercial printers are offered for the office and special devices are offered for designers and graphics artists. Finally, the company also offers digital presses that start to replace some offset printers in selected segments.

It is obvious that we have a complex structure in front of us. We apparently have consumer and commercial customers, we probably sell high-end products directly, we sell other products through the channel, we sell into all vertical markets and there should be no geographical limitation. We probably sell printers as well as aftermarket supplies, and we will have the situation that buyers are not necessarily decision makers.

In this scenario, we will have to identify a larger group of analysts and analyst firms that address the different components of our business. We will have to group them by the business they address and we will have to tier them by their respective influence. We will have to analyze if there are links and/or dependencies across analyst firms. Some firms may exchange data and thoughts on a formal or informal level. So, you may want to ensure that you treat similar companies in a similar way. It may not be appropriate, for example, to put them on different tiering levels giving them access to different service levels without a clear reason for doing so. Inviting one of them to a briefing and excluding the other one may result in a bitter aftertaste. In that case you should have a good explanation since the firm that was not invited may learn about your event and may ask questions.

Finally, we will have to check if some smaller analyst firms are for example subcontracting their services to bigger ones. This is very important information since some major analyst firms indeed gather knowledge from smaller subcontracted firms. This information becomes very relevant when tiering (i.e. prioritizing) the identified analyst firms. A company that is irrelevant at first glance may be very influential since it contributes content to major analyst firms that are very visible to customers and/or the press.

### Summary

On the previous pages we should have learned some basics for developing an industry analyst program for our company.

We probably understood that we want to work with analysts for two reasons:

Business planning: We want to be the client of an analyst firm getting consultancy from them for our own infrastructure and processes.

Industry analyst program: We want to provide the analysts with information so they can report on our company's products in the best way, i.e. in our best interest.

To identify the right analysts to work with we should look into the following questions related to our own business:

Do we sell to consumers or to commercial customers?

If commercial, which type of customers do we sell to? (Enterprises or SMBs?)

Which vertical markets do we address?

Do we sell directly or do we sell through the channel?

What geographical region do we sell in?

Does the analyst address qualitative topics like a

...detailed analysis of buying behaviors (e.g. purchase maker vs. decision maker)?

...detailed analysis of the complete value chain including the aftermarket?

The above list of questions should not only allow you to identify the right analysts for your industry analyst program, but it should also allow you right away to take a first approach on classifying the analysts in your program by their respective value for your company.

# Chapter 2:

## How Do You Reach Your Customer, or: Industry Analyst Relations In The Communication Mix

### Third-party validation

In 2002, Ed Gyurko, founder of Brand Illumination (New York) said in an interview1 that "industry analyst relations is a communications discipline based on the theory of third-party validation."

We know the power of third-party validation from various other examples.

The most obvious one may be the power of the press. It is a common belief that the press can make you immortal or it can destroy you. We may not want to go as far as giving them unlimited power like that. But it is probably fair to say that a journalist's writing can have a tremendous influence on the success or the failure of a person, an organization or a product. Film critics have a strong influence on the behavior of movie goers. Product reviews have a strong influence on customers' buying behaviors. Negative (or positive, for that matter) articles on products can have a significant effect on their sales figures. (Examples: You probably want to buy a product that is said to be an amazing bargain. But would you want to buy a bicycle helmet for your child that is said to be unsafe?)

A final proof for the value of a press endorsement is a comparison of the value of a press article with the value of an advertisement. Readers expect an advertisement to be positive on its subject. Therefore, nobody really wants to read them anymore anyway – at least not consciously. On the other hand, an article from an independent journalist could contain positive or negative statements on a product. Not only is it more fascinating to read an independent article but also is the information it contains much more objective, while an advertisement must be subjective per its definition. Media analysis theories value an article significantly higher than an advertisement – assuming they are published in the same space in the same publication. You can easily assume that an article has an influence on a reader that is up to an order of magnitude higher than that of an advertisement. – Actually, knowing that an advertisement is up to a magnitude higher in cost compared to the time and effort invested in briefing a journalist to write his article, you may really ask yourself the question why advertising as a discipline is not extinct yet…

But, there are more third-party validations than those of the press. In the following, we will discuss three other examples.

The first example is the power of celebrities giving endorsements for certain products, services or individuals. A popular actor, for example, who admits in public that

[1] The interview was done with K. Srinivasan, editor of the PRPoint Newsletter. The full interview was published in PRPoint Newsletter Vol 6 (May 2002). – Gyurko's above answer was the initial response to the question "What is industry analyst relations?

they use certain consumer products, will certainly have an impact on the demand for that product. These comments are so valuable for the manufacturer of the product that the celebrity would probably only make such positive comments after having signed a deal with the respective company to act as an ambassador for them.

An even more powerful reference is a statement from an expert who does not only act as a figure head for a marketing campaign like a celebrity may do. An expert, sometimes also referred to as a super-user, is actually using the products he comments on. An example for such an expert is a professional photographer who recommends certain cameras. Photo enthusiasts and consumers with ambitions and high standards in photography will certainly pay attention to such comments. It should be noted that experts are powerful references not only in the B2C space, but also to commercial customers.

The power of public figures endorsing products is no surprise. We can see this being exploited every day in commercials on TV. A whole industry in lifestyle PR has specialized in working with celebrities to have them say something nice about your products in public. They are courted, wined and dined, bribed or a formal contract is signed to have them stand up in public to say nice things about your products. Important in this context is the level of relationship a vendor wants to go into with a celebrity. There is a significant difference in their power to act as an advertising icon only or to be really convinced of a product and to endorse it in a non-compromising manner.

Celebrities are a powerful source for endorsements, especially in the B2C space. But a few things have to be taken into account before deciding to work with one. The value of their endorsement is certainly different than that of an industry analyst, for example. Celebrities may not be the specialists for the products they endorse. An actor endorsing certain food, for example, may only do so because they are paid to say so, and may not know the details of why this food is particularly healthy. Another aspect you should be aware of is the fact that it is a challenge to build a whole campaign on a celebrity endorsements, since you will make yourself dependent on their popularity. If the star falls, then so will your campaign.

A second example for third-party validation may not be so obvious, but we probably experience it almost every day when we go shopping. One of the most powerful endorsements actually comes from the salesperson in a shop. This person is very influential. The influence is so powerful since it happens directly at the time of purchase.

Customers who enter a shop and do not have a clear understanding yet of what product exactly they want to buy are almost certainly going to fall for the recommendation of the sales consultant in the shop. It is needless to say that companies that sell through retail depend on a strong training program to coach sales staff. Not only do they need to be trained to articulate the company's selling proposition, but often enough certain incentive schemes are introduced to influence sales personnel in retail. It is obvious that in this case this third-party validation would not be independent. Still, it is perceived as such by the customer, who tends to trust the recommendation of the sales person, especially, when he does not try to sell the most expensive item – not knowing that the sales person's measure may not be maximization of revenue, but he makes recommendations and endorses products based on profits, margins and a personal incentive scheme.

A third and final example for independent endorsements are customers themselves. In fact they turn out to be the most powerful source for third-party validation.

A satisfied customer is very likely to recommend a product or a service to friends and family. Since they know the person and since they can trust their friend such an endorsement is very convincing to them. This is especially true since the recommendation is based on experience. It is not based on academic knowledge or indirect hearsay, but on having used the product or having enjoyed a certain service. – It is important to note in this context, though, that an unsatisfied customer is an even more powerful source. Research has shown that an unsatisfied customer will spread his experience to significantly more people than a satisfied customer will share his experience.

In commercial business customer references are equally important. Corporations that sell to commercial customers often run a special customer reference program that focuses on documenting reference customers' cases and experiences. These cases will then be presented in a sales situation with a potential new customer, who will have to be convinced of the company's capabilities and of the benefits the company provides to its clients. The customer references are often also referred to as customer case studies or success stories.

We have now identified five different sources of third-party endorsements:

- Industry analysts.
- Journalists.
- Celebrities and experts.
- Sales personnel in retail.
- Customers.

It is important to note that a company could address all five groups in its marketing efforts. In doing so, a communication specialist should be aware of interaction between them.

But before we go there, we would like to stress a few points about the position of an industry analyst. He is indeed in a very special position since he brings together some characteristics of the other groups of third-parties.

Since an analyst works a lot with customers, he acts as a "super customer". His opinion represents the opinion of dozens or hundreds of customers. His experience is based on the experience of many customers. Thus, he does not just represent a single experience that may be statistically irrelevant, but their validation is based on a sample that makes their findings so much more powerful.

At the same time, industry analysts tend to have a good technical understanding of the topics they address. In that capacity they appear to the customer in a similar light as the sales consultant in a shop – with the big advantage that the industry analyst is truly independent, i.e. he is not on an incentive scheme of any vendor.

Also, analysts operate similar to the press. Either they communicate to the public via the press or they have their own communication vehicles like newsletters or special reports that are distributed widely. In some cases, the border line between the analyst community and the press community is blurring. Some analysts tend to behave very similar to journalists and some journalists try to position themselves similar to analysts. In this context it is interesting to position the business analysts that are often enough employed by major business publications. The way you work with them will depend a lot on the objectives you define for your analyst program (see also the section on industry analysts and journalists in chapter 3).

And finally, you can argue that industry analysts can today be considered to be celebrities in the business world. Their word counts. They are in a unique position allowing them to collect information like probably nobody else in the industry. Customers value their inputs very highly.

We now want to have a look into the interaction between the different parties we discussed. All parties can be positioned to be located somewhere between the initial vendor and the customers. Graphically, links can be shown as in the following diagram:



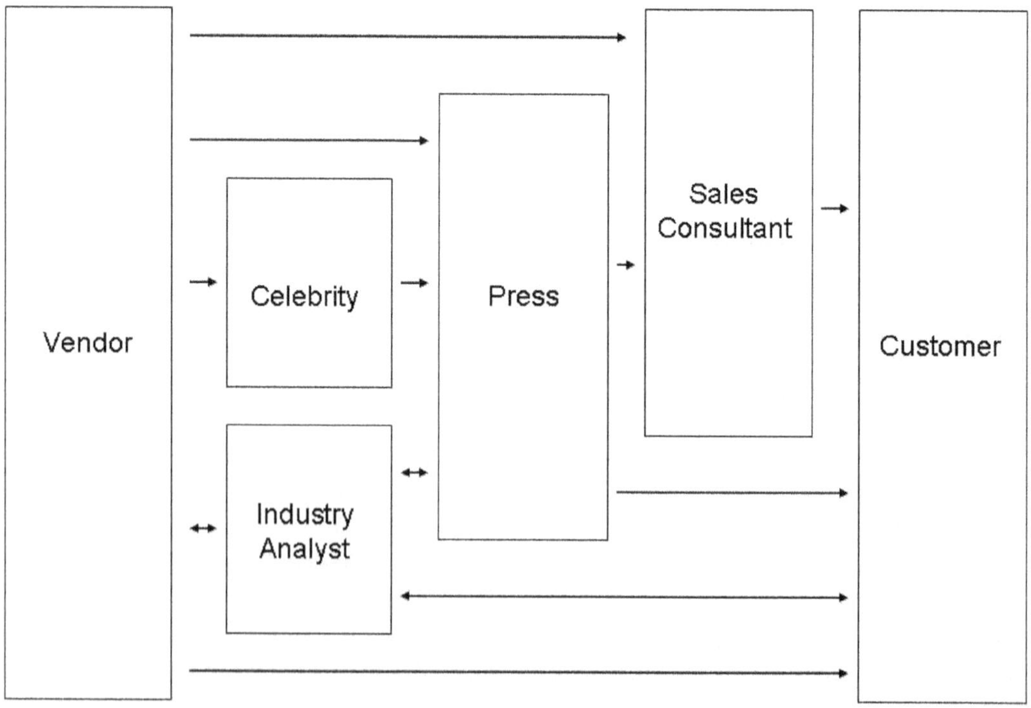


Figure 2.1: Vendor-customer communication

While all communication tends to go from the vendor towards the customer, it is interesting to note that the communication lines of the industry analysts indicate a true communication rather than just an information transfer in one direction.

It should also be recognized that industry analysts are probably the most influential group in the above diagram providing input to the customer directly as well as influencing other influencers.

The above diagram shows that a company must align its outbound communication well, since the individual parties are not independent but interconnected. This would not imply that messages have to be identical for all target audiences, but they certainly have to be coordinated. In other words, a journalist should hear a consistent story from a company's PR department and from an industry analyst. The analyst, in return, may receive a dedicated briefing. Still, the information he received is consistent with the information the journalist received in a press release, an interview or a press conference.1

A simple example: A journalist would only be told the benefits of a new product. The story is kept simple to get the main message across very clearly. An analyst, however, would not only be informed about the new product's highlights. An analyst would also be interested in learning about the detailed product features and benefits and about what is actually going on inside the box. Therefore, an analyst briefing would also cover an update on the technology. This, in return, would allow the analyst to drive conclusions about not only the current product, but also about the future. For example, a product that is based on a new technology should have a growth path ahead of it to allow for future upgrades and ongoing support. On the other hand, if the product is based on an older technology then the company may have to do a roll-over of its product line soon. The implication for the analyst is clear: He may not want to recommend the old technology to a customer who creates a new infrastructure for future growth. However, he may want to recommend it to a customer who requires a cost effective point solution only.

Another example is a bit more complex. Again, we want to keep a message simple and straightforward with the press. We position a new product for the major markets we want to address, but we do not distract the press discussing also potential new niche markets. With analysts we may want to go into these details. Maybe we can even get access to these niche markets through the analysts. If we are not decided yet if we really want to address the new markets and if we do the analyst briefings early enough, we may even want to discuss our thoughts and intentions with the analysts openly and seek their feedback – before we actually make a final decision to ultimately invest in addressing these niches. The analysts' feedback would then help us make a decision if we want to invest in addressing new markets after all.

---

[1] In this context it is important to note that it is actually the expressed expectation of analysts not to be treated in the way as journalists. They may go to press conferences from time to time. But the event is not necessarily their primary source for information. But it is useful for them to go there from time to time to verify that a company's messaging is consistent. In briefings for themselves they would certainly expect additional information like a company's overall strategy, a company's go-to-market approach or additional background information.

The need to coordinate content and message is obvious. But a company's communication department needs to go beyond that. Crucial is also timing. When new information is disclosed to the public, i.e. to the press, industry analysts should already be aware of the news. In other words: Industry analyst briefings need to happen before press embargo dates. There are two reasons for that. The first one is to provide analysts with sufficient time to digest the news and to form an opinion on it. The second one is to allow them to be available for interviews with the press, once they seek second opinions on the information they just received from a vendor – and, of course, to be available with comments for their client base immediately after a public announcement.

### Investor relations

In the previous sub-chapter we have seen how industry analysts are embedded in a network of influencers addressing customers. We have also seen implications for a company's communication strategy to address all influencer communities in a consistent way.

We now want to have a look into a different audience, a corporation tends to address as part of its communication mix: Investors.

Every public corporation runs an investor relations program of some sort. In a classical approach, corporations are interested in a balanced scorecard addressing customers, investors and employees.

While industry analysts only have a limited impact on a company's employees1 they certainly have a strong influence on investors' opinions – even though they hardly ever speak directly to them.

Investors are typically receiving their information either directly from a company through its investor relations program, or they receive information from financial analysts. Financial analysts (also referred to as security analysts) also get briefed by a corporation's investor relations program. This information allows them to draw conclusions on a company's financial situation, they can do financial projections, and they can do comparisons with industry benchmarks. Financial analysts are brilliant in interpreting earnings announcements, but they typically struggle to understand technology. Therefore, they depend on a sounding board helping them to form an opinion on a company's future growth potential based on their strategic directions, new product capabilities and technology positioning.

It is probably no surprise that industry analysts again come into the picture. It turns out that there is a loose network between financial analysts and industry analysts sharing findings with each other. we have described that financial analysts need the help of industry analysts to interpret the value of and the opportunities for certain

---

[1] You may want to boost employees' morale by having industry analysts do an internal presentation to them that points out the company's strength. It is always better to hear this from an external source than from an internal executive, who employees may not expect another message from anyway.

technologies. But industry analysts, in return, are also very interested in the opinion of financial analysts. In order to provide their clients with a complete picture and in order to consult with them properly, they would not only address technical aspects. They would also need to pay attention to recommending solutions to their clients that are provided by a financially sound organization to secure long lasting support, future extensions and upgrades. An enterprise will always take a supplier's financial stability into consideration, since there is too much at stake. Contracts with IT suppliers could easily be worth tens of millions of dollars. Enterprises want to ensure that this investment is safe, i.e. the supplier does not go out of business tomorrow nor does it change strategy away from the products they have just bought – and ideally they also look for second sourcing to minimize risks even further.

A diagram showing the influencer network towards investors looks a bit simpler than the one we have seen earlier addressing customers:

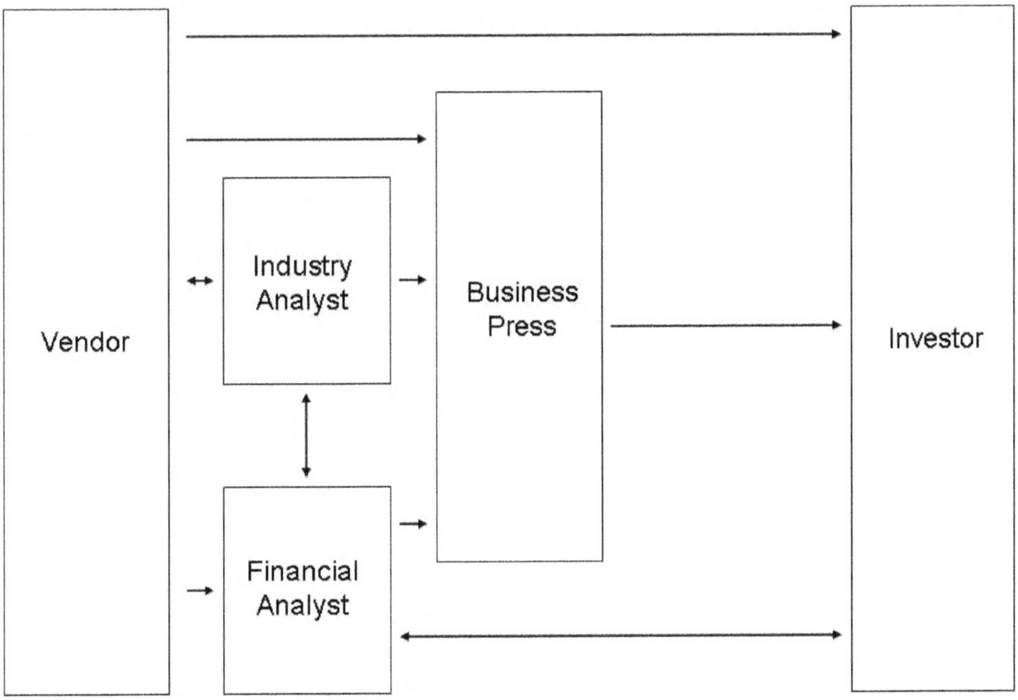


Figure 2.2: Vendor-investor communication

Again we see that industry analysts play an important role in this "ecosystem".

But, we also see that the press is part of the picture again. In this case, however, it is not generically the entire press, but it is specifically the business press. The business press tends to have good links both to financial analysts and to industry analysts. For example, you will find quotes in the Financial Times or in the Wall Street Journal from companies like Merrill Lynch, but also from analyst firms like Gartner.

And, it is interesting to note in this context that some industry analyst firms in fact run an incentive program for their analysts to get themselves quoted in selected publications, primarily business publications. This clearly shows their ambition to be an influential source being heard loud and clear in communities where they may recruit their next clients.

### Industry Analyst Relations and Marcom

The term "Marcom" for Marketing Communications is used in many corporations today. It is sometimes misleading since it suggests that the Marcom team looks after all communication of the corporation. In reality this is not necessarily the case. Advertising is often enough managed as a separate discipline, and so is PR. Internal communications (or: employee communication) is also often treated separately.

Marcom tends to focus nowadays on the development of sales collateral. This would include direct marketing materials (see detailed section below) and standard sales literature like product data sheets, brochures, leaflets, etc. Packaging would be part of the Marcom discipline as well.

In this section we want to highlight only briefly the interaction Marcom may have with Industry Analyst Relations.

In selected sales materials it may be appropriate to show off third party endorsements. Typically with consumer and SMB solutions this would be product awards or product test results like in Consumer Reports, Which? or, in Germany, from the popular Stiftung Warentest. There may also be quotes from celebrities or experts. In some cases it may also be appropriate to include a statement from an industry analyst in the brochure. In that case the Marcom department would work closely with the Industry Analyst Relations team to get the statement approved from the analyst firm for public use. Note that the right to use the quote or diagram may be subject to a charge.

We will discuss the special case of developing jointly branded collateral with analysts in the next sub-chapter.

A Marcom department may also be interested to integrate analysts into customer events the company may want to organize. Analysts make excellent guest speakers addressing topics that you want to address by a neutral source rather than by a company spokesperson. It should be much more credible to have an analyst talk about trends in the industry, for example. If that was done by a company speaker there would always be some suspicion that he only wants to talk about trends that the company can actually address ignoring a complete picture of the developments in the market.

### Industry analyst relations and direct marketing

Industry analysts typically have two different sets of clients. They consult with users and they consult with vendors. Knowing the power of their role and potentially the power of their respective brand, many industry analyst firms also make themselves available for joint marketing activities with vendors. In doing so, they obviously walk on a thin line. They run the risk of being dragged too closely to a vendor, i.e. they would lose their neutral status. They cannot allow that to happen, since their credibility is obviously their biggest asset.1

Nevertheless, some analyst firms even run dedicated programs to develop joint and co-branded collateral with vendors. Their contribution to the joint material is not so much an endorsement of the vendor's opinions and products, but their independent view of the industry and most and for all the power of their brand.

The material would serve as a newsletter to customers, as direct marketing collateral to potential leads, as handout material at trade shows or conferences or simply as background material at any kind of events.

Joint programs with analysts tend to be very powerful. Just put yourself into the shoes of an IT manager of a major corporation. You receive a mailing from a vendor X on their latest range of networking solutions. Most likely, your conclusion will be that this is just another advertisement and the envelope will end up in the bin soon afterwards. Now assume you receive a document from a popular analyst firm Y and a vendor X on the future of networking. There is a much higher likelihood that you will pay attention to this document and read it – even though it will contain product news from vendor X as well and serve a very similar purpose as the above advertisement.

Collateral as described above typically allows customers to respond in some way. Either they fill in an order right away, or they respond to an invitation to an event, or they can request additional information or they simply participate in a raffle. It shows that response rates to collateral done jointly with analysts are significantly higher than those of "normal" direct mailing pieces. Typically the increase justifies the higher investment in the cooperation with the analyst firm.

But even if a full blown joint activity is not considered, industry analysts can still enrich a company's communication material to its clients. Approved quotes or references from analysts can give a vendor's announcement or statement more weight. Important to note is that the quote must be approved by the analyst firm before using it. It would not be sufficient to simply quote e.g. from an analyst's research note. A research note is not in the public domain like e.g. a press article, but it is available to paying clients only and typically restrictions apply to the use of its content, even though it may be referenced properly. The same obviously applies to the use of analyst quotes in advertisements.

### Industry analyst relations and PR

Public relations departments have discovered the power of working with analysts a long time ago already. The close link between PR and IAR (industry analyst relations) often enough stirs the discussion where an industry analyst relations team should ac-

[1] See also appendix A.

tually reside within a corporation. An obvious approach may be to run the program from within the PR department. For smaller organizations with only limited resources this may indeed be the only valid option. For larger corporations, however, different options could be considered. One option is to run an analyst relations program in parallel to a PR program, both reporting to the same function, a marketing manager, Chief Marketing Officer, or directly to the CEO. Both options are reasonable. Which one to select depends on the size of the company and the importance of industry analyst relations to the organization. The only word of caution we would raise, though, is to ensure that analyst relations continues to use its own toolset and processes, when embedded into a PR team.

A third option may be to have financial analyst and industry analyst relations combined, while PR continues to be a separate organization being closely aligned with the other marketing communication functions. we might consider this option if the company is mainly interested in investor relations. In real life, though, we have not come across a scenario where this approach would be the best solution.

After this brief diversion we want to return to the links between PR and analyst relations. There are many opportunities to exploit analyst findings in PR.

A common example is to issue a press release on recent market share data published by an analyst firm. It is obviously a strong message supporting a company's strategy if an analyst firm confirms the company's market leadership or its growth rates.

At the same time it should be said that this kind of press announcement is massively overused in several industries, in particular in the IT industry. The news value of a monthly or quarterly announcement trumpeting the most recent market share data out can become very questionable. Such a press release often ends up adding to the background noise of information ending up on a journalist's desk on a daily basis. It is very likely that the journalist will ignore it.

But industry analysts offer much more to PR than just providing market share data. They can obviously provide a reference for a new product. Typically this would not be an appraisal of the product, but for example a more sophisticated approach mapping product benefits to certain customer demands. Such approach would be more in line with their neutral status. Analysts can also provide insight to market trends. They can directly or indirectly endorse a company's strategy. The most important thing is that they are always seen as an independent source. Comments from an analyst can always be referred to as a second opinion. Thus, if such a quote is provided by a vendor right away with the announcement it saves the journalist time searching for a comment on the announcement.1

In a similar way it has become a common procedure to invite analysts to speak at press conferences directly to the press. Again, it is important to note that their role would not be to endorse a new product or service, for example. Their role would

1 Even though a good journalist will not replace his own investigation by a prepared statement, it is a sad fact that time pressure often enough forces journalists to be inventive.

rather be to discuss the market and trends in the market. They can also comment on a company's strategy with respect to market trends or industry dynamics. However, analysts would hardly spoil their reputation as an independent body by providing a blunt appraisal for a new product at a press conference. If they still do so, then they are either genuinely excited and convinced – or they are bribed.

When inviting analysts to speak at press conferences, vendors walk a fine line. They obviously would like to control what the analyst is going to say, but they cannot "misuse" them by dictating to them what to say.

We have made the experience that taking risks pays back! In other words: You need to be confident in what your company brings to market and you need to be confident that you have briefed the analyst well. If your product is really as powerful as you think or if your company's strategy really makes sense then an analyst who was invited to speak at your press conference will say so and support your view, or at least he will not go against it and complement your spokespeople's speeches appropriately.

At an international press conference a few years ago one of us invited an analyst to be part of a panel discussion that was led by an external host. So, neither the analyst nor the host was directly controlled by the organizing company. Since the conversation was not rehearsed – and since this became very obvious to the audience – it was received very well by the participating members of the press. They understood that they did not watch a prepared stage play, but they followed an open exchange of ideas. The coverage in the press was very positive after this event.

We believe in the power of such an open approach, since we need to assume that journalists would get the information they are after anyway. A PR manager would hardly be able to hide information a journalist could get from other sources like from industry analysts. He would not be able to control the communication between a journalist and an analyst. This conversation could take place still at the press conference in a 1:1 interview or offline after the event.

Even if you do not invite analysts directly to a press conference a communication between the two would take place anyway. We have mentioned above already that journalists and industry analysts not only know each other, but they tend to exchange information on a regular basis. we guess it is fair to say that most journalists have a list of their favorite analysts they could call if they have questions or if they need second opinions on news they initially heard elsewhere.

As already mentioned before, an obvious implication from the above is that analysts need to be briefed before the press is informed. Exact timing would depend on lead times of the announcing company and on general time frames in the industry the company is in. In the IT industry we have the experience that it is appropriate to brief analysts a few weeks or at least a few days before the communication to the press – a few hours notice is considered to be too short for many analysts. Passing on new information to analysts about one month prior to a press announcement would give analysts sufficient time to digest the news and form an opinion on it. The analysts could prepare so-called "first takes" on the news announcement in advance and could publish them on the announcement day complying with the embargo date or with agreed NDAs (non-disclosure agreements).

### Industry analyst relations and business planning

Corporations tend to have two interests in working closely with industry analysts. The business planning team is interested in receiving information from analysts that helps them to plan ahead. And the analyst relations team is interested in providing analysts with the appropriate information to allow them to form an opinion on the company, its strategy and its offerings.

Both these links between the analyst community and a corporation follow separate processes. Both communication paths should be kept separate to avoid potential conflicts of interest. Even though analyst firms tend to point out very clearly that they do not prefer a vendor because he happens to be their client and even though vendors tend to point out clearly that they do not bribe analysts, an interdependency between vendor and analyst can never be excluded. It should be obvious that such a behavior is not only unethical, but could also be extremely damaging if it was ever revealed. It would be damaging for an analyst if it is revealed that he favors a certain vendor because he happens to be their client. And it would also be damaging to a vendor if it became public that he "buys" analyst opinions.

A Business Planning Team or a Business Intelligence Team is typically the client of an analyst. They would purchase their research and integrate the information into their plans. In this communication path the information would mainly flow from the analyst to the corporation.

An Analyst Relations Team would be responsible for feeding company information to the analysts. The main information flow would be from the corporation to the industry analyst in this case.1

Both teams would obviously work together. For example, they should exchange information on the relative importance of the analyst firms they work together with. "Importance" may be measured differently by both entities, though. While the planning team is interested in the analyst firm's knowledge, the analyst relations team is interested in the analyst firm's customer base and the influence they have on end users.

Their respective counterparts in the analyst firm, the sales department and the analysts themselves, would work together as well. Typically, the analysts would consult with the planning team directly while the sales team manages the communication.

---

[1] This sentence should not imply that the communication with analysts is a one way street in analyst relations. Quite the contrary! We want to exploit the program to maintain a true dialog with analysts and we certainly want to get feedback and listen to opinions that can be very valuable indeed for the company's planning. Analysts can act as a sounding board for message testing or simply have an open dialogue with company representatives – even though the company may not be one of their formal clients.

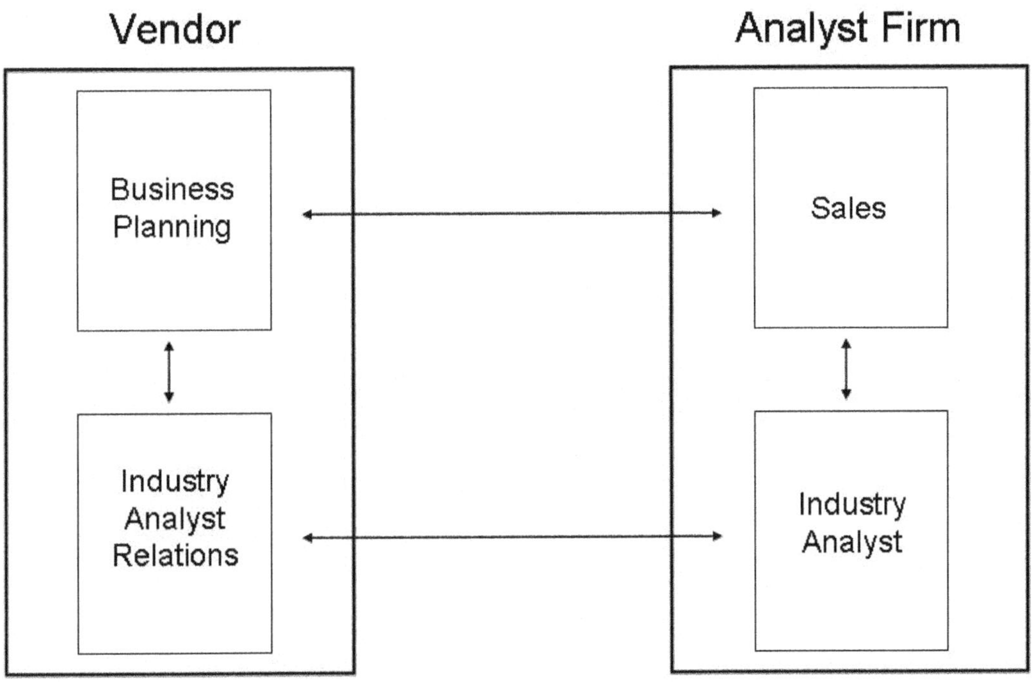


Figure 2.3: Vendor-analyst firm communication

**Summary**

The communication discipline Industry Analyst Relations is a very valuable one for a corporation. We have seen that the corporation would benefit significantly from close ties to all other communication disciplines.

Close cooperation between the communication disciplines would not only align all outbound communication, it would also ensure that the corporation can benefit from potential leverage effects.

We have discussed a few examples in this chapter. we should mention that the above does not address all potential links. Just like we have seen we can benefit from industry analyst statements in Marcom, in PR or in Direct Marketing, we should be prepared to consider the usage of analyst comments also in other disciplines like in advertising or in company internal (employee) communication. External statements e.g. from analysts could be very powerful to lift the morale of the workforce, analyst presentations in coffee talks or in virtual internal presentations (e.g. via the intranet) could not only be motivating, but could also be used to train the employees - or they can be used as a supporting tool to address change management. It should be mentioned that a very good use of industry analysts is their involvement in sales force trainings.

The following diagram summarizes the disciplines in the Communication or Marketing department we want the Industry Analyst Program to interact with.

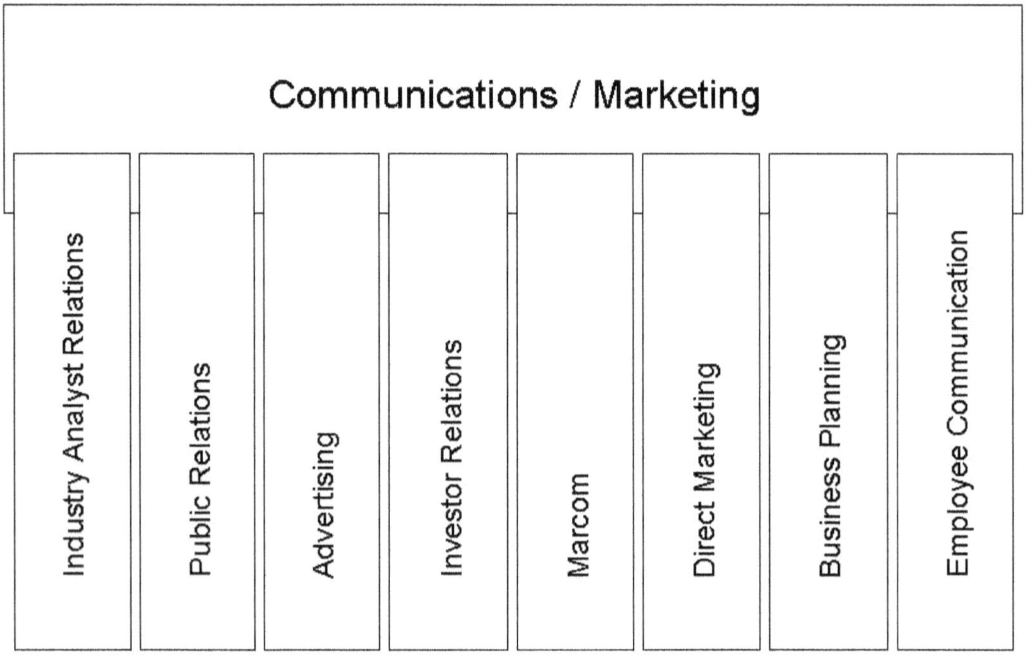


Figure 2.4: Communication mix

## Chapter 3:

## What Is An Industry Analyst?

Even though the title of this chapter sounds like a simple question, it is actually not. The definition of an analyst is certainly not straightforward. This is partly because most analysts would define their own respective roles differently. we guess, if you asked four industry analysts how they would describe their job you would get five different answers.

It is also because there are in fact very different types of analysts. Some analysts consult with users, some with vendors. Some analysts focus on qualitative customer benefits, some focus on quantitative market share data.

And finally, it is because the border between the job description of an analyst and that of a neighboring job is not necessarily well defined. There are gray areas between industry analysts and financial analysts. There are gray areas between industry analysts and journalists. And, just ask yourself what the difference is between an industry analyst and a consultant. We will answer most of these questions later in this chapter.

We will also have a look into the details of what an industry analyst actually is in this chapter. There will be several learnings from the following pages. They include:

- The ability to define an analyst.
- The ability to select the right analysts into an analyst relations program.
- The ability to sort analysts by certain criteria.
- The ability to tier (i.e. prioritize) analysts.
- The ability to de-select individuals from an industry analyst relations program.

We mentioned earlier that we want to include analysts who influence our customers into our industry analyst program. Unfortunately, not all industry analysts actually work with our customers. And – to confuse things even further, there are individuals in analyst firms who also work with our customers, but we may not want to include them into our analyst program for reasons we will explain below.

### Analysts – sorted by their clients

Industry analysts can be sorted by their respective client base. There are analyst firms that focus their services on users, i.e. typically on enterprises. Their goal is to collect as much information on the market, on trends, on news from vendors, etc to help their clients to make the right purchasing decisions.

On the other side of the spectrum are analyst firms who predominantly serve vendors. These companies typically sell market share data or market research to vendors to help them make the right planning decisions. This would include all decisions from forecasting product demand to defining strategic directions.

Major analyst houses like Gartner or IDC tend to have both disciplines in house. They serve users as well as vendors. Traditional Gartner analysts, for example, were always more focused on users. With the acquisition of Dataquest, Gartner also brought a strong entity into the organization that focused their service more on vendors.

It is recommended to sort all analysts at some time based on their client structure. A result may look like this:

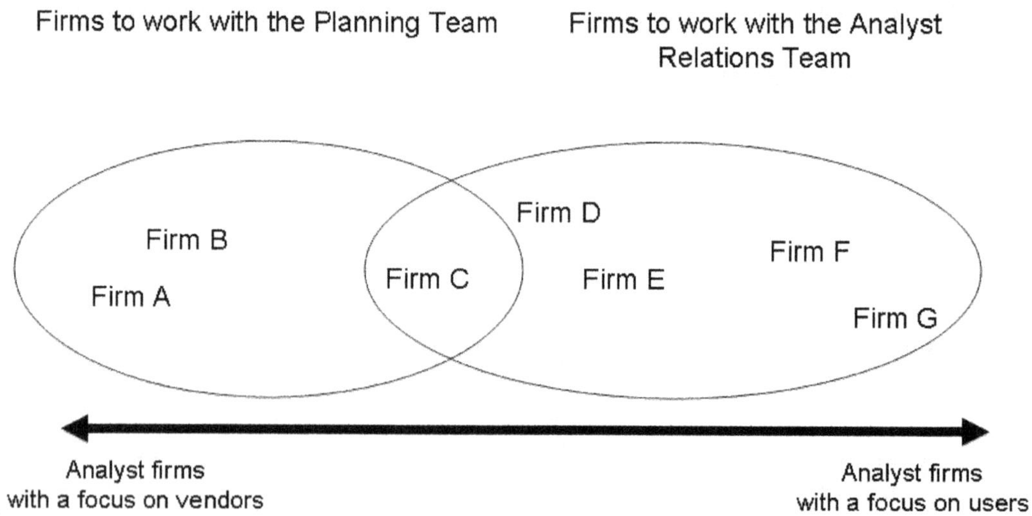


Figure 3.1: Analysts – sorted by their clients

We can derive several conclusions from this diagram.

On the left hand side of the diagram we will find the analyst firms that are relevant for our planning or business intelligence department to work with. This department may decide to purchase the analyst firm's research, get access to their services like consulting, newsletters, opinion pieces, etc.

On the right hand side we will find those analyst firms that influence our customers, i.e. those analysts that we want to work with in our industry analyst relations program.

Analyst firms in the middle of the spectrum are having a mixed client structure. It ranges from being dominated by users to being dominated by vendors. For those firms we may want to do the sorting exercise again, but this time we want to sort the individual analysts by their focus areas. We should find that some of them are more focused on users and some others are more focused on working with vendors. All analysts have a very clear set of measures that defines their role. Their salaries are typically dependent on how well they sell their time to their clients (being users, vendors or a mix). And they tend to have defined target audiences or they have a clear preference either to work with vendors or to work with users.

**Analysts – sorted by their tasks**

In this subchapter we want to look a bit closer into the tasks of an individual industry analyst. We have seen before that not all industry analysts share the same job description and the same measures. we will try to segment the analyst community into a few groups that represent the most common analyst types.

The following diagram provides an overview of the five groups we will discuss below:

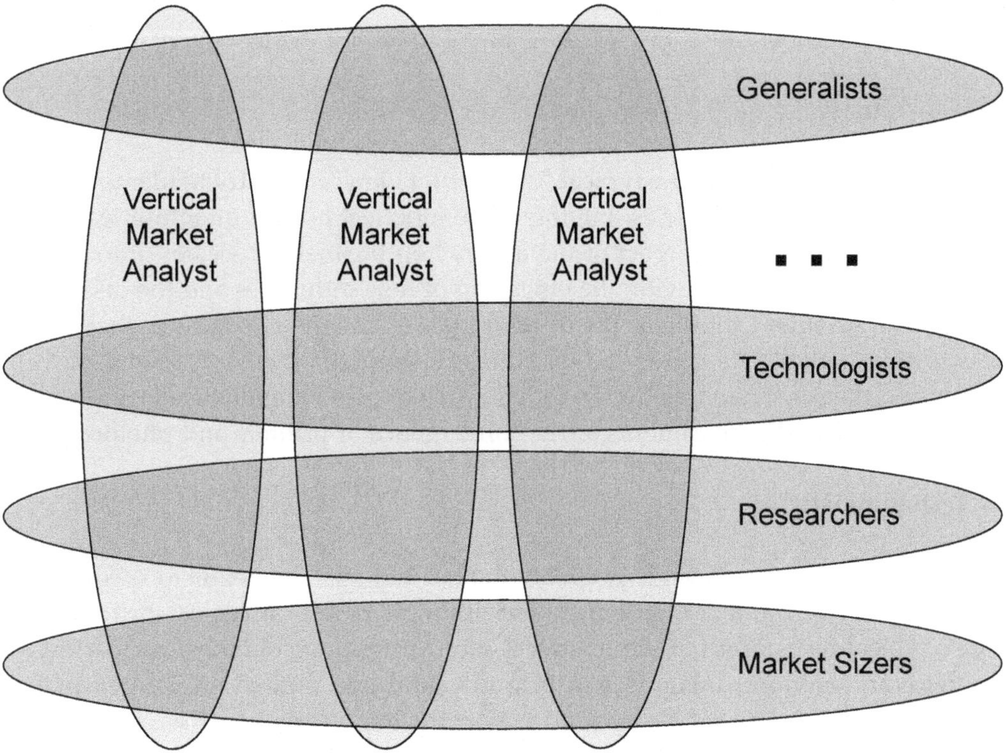


Figure 3.2: Analysts – sorted by their tasks "Market sizers"

Market sizers develop the basis for most of the work done by others. They collect shipment data from vendors and from retailers. They segment the market. They provide data to show historical trends. Market sizers basically compile a huge data set that shows the dynamics in the industry. Market sizers per definition mainly look backwards. You can obviously extrapolate into the future from their data, but this task is either done by other analysts, or it is done by planning departments in corporations. Market sizers provide only very limited value to our organization. Typically, a vendor purchases market share data from one or two analyst firms – and in return supports them with data. But it is more than questionable if the vendor wants to invest into supporting analysts that he does not buy the consolidated data back from. For an analyst relations program, these analysts are not the prime targets. An industry analyst relations program would certainly have a different focus.

**"Researchers"**

Researchers try to find answers to questions that have been handed over to them by their clients or that they want to have answered for the industry generically. The task could be to compare solutions from different vendors for specific challenges. The task could also be to determine customers' buying behavior or any other question that people and institutions want answers for – and are willing to pay money for.

**"Generalists"**

Generalists tend to have the typical "30,000 foot view". They try to identify global trends like changes in industries, buying behaviors, technology quantum leaps, etc. A typical example was the impact of the internet on business processes, information flow, customers' buying behavior, the emerging of new industries and the disappearing of others. Another example is the development of mobile IT solutions that allows access to information like never before. A final example is the convergence of technologies and the consequences for the industry (examples include the convergence of mobile phones and digital cameras or the convergence of printers and photocopiers).

**"Technologists"**

The most common analyst is probably the technologist. He tends to specialize in a certain technology and compare different offerings based on typical customer demands. Typical focus areas of these analysts are computing solutions, network solutions, telecom solutions, imaging and printing solutions, and so on. Larger analyst firms can afford to have analysts specialize even further on areas such as storage solutions, database software solutions, services and support or commercial printing solutions.

**"Vertical market analysts"**

Several analyst firms exclusively focus on special vertical markets (e.g. Heavy Reading on the telecoms industry, InfoTrends on imaging and printing or Manufacturing Insights on the manufacturing segment) or have departments that focus on special vertical markets like e.g. the automotive industry, the telecom industry, the financial sector or the pharmaceutical industry. These analysts are specialists. Their needs are significantly different from that of a technologist. If analysts addressing vertical markets and technologists are addressed by a single industry analyst program the program owner must be aware of their respective demands. A technologist tends to be sufficiently informed as long as he receives all product features of a new product a vendor brings to market. A vertical market analyst, however, always thinks in terms of benefits for the clients in the respective segment or market. For example, a vertical market analyst would not be interested in the raw performance data of a computer as measured e.g. in MFLOPS. He would rather be interested in the number of transactions the platform can do using a certain financial software.

### Analysts – sorted by their regional responsibility

Many analyst firms follow a hierarchy. The highest layer of analysts has a worldwide responsibility. They coordinate the analyst work on a global basis. In particular, they pay attention to aligning the firm's opinions across the globe.

The next layer of analysts has a regional responsibility. Typically, there are four to five worldwide regions:

- North America (USA and Canada):
  Sometimes Canada is addressed as a separate region.
- Latin America
- EMEA (Europe, Middle East, Africa)
  Often split into Western Europe and the developing countries.
- Asia-Pacific

In some cases Australia and Japan are independent since their economies cannot be compared to emerging markets in the region like e.g. India or China.

The final layer consists of analysts who address individual countries.

The owner of an industry analyst program needs to ensure that he includes analysts with the right scope into their program. Otherwise he could end up with one of the following scenarios:

The scope of the analyst program is for EMEA, but a participating analyst is responsible for Italy only. The message delivered in the program is true for EMEA as a whole, but the market in Italy happens to be different. In this case the Italian analyst could be misled.

The scope of the analyst program is for the UK, but a participating analyst is responsible for Western Europe. It turns out that the company running the analyst program is only emerging in Europe, and so far is present in the UK only. Again, the analyst could be misled doing wrong extrapolations to the rest of Europe.

The scope of the analyst program is EMEA with a strong focus on Western Europe. A participating analyst from Russia will either be misled by the messages, or he will be bored since the messages are not relevant for their region.

A corporation that runs industry analyst programs on multiple geographical levels needs to ensure that the analysts receive information that is relevant for their respective work.

There are additional aspects caused by geographical responsibilities. Messages shared with analysts in North America, for example, need to be consistent with messages shared in Europe. In fact, international analyst firms often enough take advantage of the fact that their analysts can participate in several briefings. It is an opportunity for them to check a company's message for consistency.

### Analysts and consultants

We have asked the question already in the introduction to this chapter: What is the difference between an analyst and a consultant. The answer will not be very satisfying, since it will be a typical one along the lines of "it depends".

One approach trying to define the difference between the two would be to characterize an analyst as a more academic individual, while a consultant applies the generic knowledge to specific customer cases. In fact, this approach is not too far from the truth, so we want to take this as a first iteration.

Analyst firms often enough employ both, industry analysts and consultants. The analyst is indeed the individual who collects all information. He then develops an opinion on the information and documents it in research notes, newsletters or other collateral. He would be available to present the findings for example at conferences or in strategic presentations to clients. He would not be available to take the information and apply it to a specific problem of a client. Such a specific problem would be owned by a consultant.

We will look at an example:

An industry analyst is responsible for enterprise computing solutions. He looks into typical solutions for corporate and departmental datacenters. He is familiar with all major vendors' offerings. This would include hardware, software and services. He would also be informed about the companies' future plans, cooperation between companies, prices, and so on. Based on all this information the analyst would be able to compare available offerings and he would be able to provide clients with a recommendation what products and vendors to consider in an upcoming purchase.

A customer who is for example interested to change its database infrastructure would be able to consult with the analyst on what to include in an RFP (request for proposal) and what vendors to approach for a proposal.

If the same customer then also requires support or project management of the actual implementation, he would get a consultant involved. Interestingly enough, analyst firms often also provide that service. They would provide project management or in-depth consultancy on specific projects. Those consultants would then implement the customer's project, for example work out a detailed project plan to change that database infrastructure we mentioned above. An industry analyst is hardly ever involved in a client's project on that level.

However, the borders between analysts and consultant are blurring. Especially in smaller analyst firms and in firms that consult with SMB customers, analysts are typically more involved in project management. You may sometimes even ask the question if they can still be called analysts or if they fall more into the "consultant category". Analysts who specialize in very narrow niche markets also have a tendency to operate both, as an analyst and as a consultant.

We have seen analysts who consult with a very small number of mid-sized companies on very special IT projects. These analysts run typical analyst services to a wider audience, but they also do in-depth project management for their clients.

So, why do we actually worry about the difference between analysts and consultants? Shouldn't we include analysts as well as consultants in our industry analyst program?

The answer is a very clear no. – We certainly want to be flexible with those smaller firms. We may want to include them into our program, but we have them on a lower tiering level, i.e. we may provide only limited services to them, or we keep them at a lower priority level.

Consultants from larger analyst firms should typically not be part of the industry analyst program. In those companies the analysts typically operate as the gatekeeper to new information coming from vendors. The analysts are the influential individuals. They are the ones to digest information from vendors and other organizations and finally form an opinion on them. Analyst firms normally have a very strong interest in coming to a single company wide opinion that is shared across all employees. It would look strange if one analyst had a different opinion on the same topic as one of their colleagues from the same company. All analysts in the company are part of the process of forming that opinion – the consultants are typically not part of it.

Since an industry analyst relations program is measured against the success of influencing the influencers, analysts need to be in its focus and not consultants. Consultants would get their guidance from analysts – and are typically not briefed directly by vendors.

As always, exceptions apply, but typically consultants would not be addressed by a company's industry analyst program. One reason is information control within the analyst firm. Another reason is based on the fact that consultants tend to operate more on a local level. While many analysts look after an entire region like North America or EMEA (Europe, Middle East, Africa), a consultant often operates within a country or in an even narrower environment.

Consultants typically have a different link to equipment vendors they get involved with in their projects: They tend to work closely with the local sales and support organization.

An analyst relations manager also has an interest in keeping the number of consultants in their program as low as possible. As we have seen earlier, industry analysts tend to receive information way before a public embargo date. In theory they would have to sign a non-disclosure agreement (NDA) in return for getting information that early. Some companies insist on having an NDA signed before a briefing, some others provide the information based on a gentlemen's agreement. In return for giving the analysts information early, the analysts will not publish the news before the public embargo date.

We personally favor the informal communication, i.e. we would not insist on having an NDA signed – unless it is the employer's policy to do so. It shows that an informal approach provides the right basis for open discussions between industry analysts and representatives from a vendor's company. And we have never seen an analyst breach such a verbal agreement! This approach, however, requires us to select the participants in such a briefing and in the industry analyst program very carefully. Consultants, who tend to be very close to their clients, and other individuals who would not qualify as industry analysts may be potential leaks before the public announcement of the news you want to share.

### Industry analysts and journalists

On paper, there is a clear difference between an industry analyst and a journalist. In real life, though, there is a significant gray area between both job descriptions.

A journalist is not necessarily a specialist in a topic like an industry analyst. Journalists tend to be more generalists – especially in the changing media landscape where less and less journalists need to fill the pages of newspapers and magazines across a broad range of topics. Analysts tend to be specialists in comparatively narrow fields of interest – exceptions apply. For example, while an analyst may specialize in storage solutions only, a journalist may need to cover processor technologies today and gaming consoles tomorrow.

Both analysts and journalists have a few things in common, though. They both share their information with users. Journalists do so writing about the news in the press. Analysts tend to share their information in research notes or on a 1:1 basis with users. However, several analyst firms also publish regular newsletters for their clients – and they publish news flashes as needed.

As soon as the subscription to the news flashes becomes a significant part of the analyst firm's revenue, the involved analysts run the risk of adopting the behavior of a journalist: They want to run news as soon as possible. This obviously runs the involved industry analysts into a conflict of interest. Because of their role as an industry analyst they tend to receive information way before a journalist ever learns about it. But they need to comply with the embargo date the organization that delivered the news has set. In other words: They have information they know would make excellent news in their newsletter now. And if they published it now they would give their readers an advantage over those users who will only receive it from other sources after the embargo date.

It is needless to say that it must be very tempting to ignore the embargo date and to publish the news right away. Every industry analyst knows that their position is dependent on being accepted by users in general, and particularly by their clients. But he also knows that there is a dependency also on vendors and other sources in the industry. Therefore, every analyst knows that violating agreements could make them a persona non grata in future briefings. He would be cut off from information, which is probably the most severe punishment for an analyst. Information is the life line.

Most analysts would honor embargo dates and share confidential information only as advised by the person or the organization that shared it in the first place. But, there are indeed some "black sheep" around, that behave like journalists and would not honor the confidentiality of something like an "off the record" discussion. Especially the analysts working for business publications fall into this group. Their job title is indeed analyst, however they work for a publishing house. Even though they are not necessarily journalists writing articles themselves, they do the research for their publishing colleagues.

These analysts should not be included in a company's industry analyst relations program. Or, at least they should not be treated in the same way as analysts who comply with certain ground rules and with verbal gentlemen's agreements. These analysts may be treated just like "normal" representatives from the press, i.e. they would be invited to press conferences only or they would be on the distribution list for press releases and other information for the press.

In some cases it is unavoidable to brief analysts and the press simultaneously. Examples include the announcements of mergers and acquisitions. In these cases it is appropriate to invite both audiences to the same event, e.g. a press conference or a phone based briefing. In general, however, both audiences should be separated to maximize the value for the respective groups. Saving money may not be a good reason for addressing press and analysts in one go. The results may backfire on you. If analysts receive the information at the same time as journalists, for example, they would not be able to reflect on the news sufficiently to provide proper quotes to the press. While this may be considered to be a minor issue, there is a much more direct impact on your business caused by briefing analysts only late: The analysts would not have been able to consider your new offering when consulting with their clients. Note that long decision cycles would allow them to guide their clients accordingly – without actually pre-announcing your new offering to them.

### Industry analysts and other influencers

The objective of an industry analyst relations program is – to put it very bluntly – to influence the influencers.

An obvious question would be why you want to limit yourself to just influencing industry analysts. Why not include other influencers into your program?

It is obvious that you want to work with all influencers – as long as your bandwidth allows you to do so. But you must reconsider the idea to address all of them with the same program. Reality is that the approach with a single program will not work.

There are several reasons why you need to separate different audiences.

Celebrities are influencers for consumer goods. Industry analysts can also influence consumers with statements they make in public about products or services. Still, celebrities and industry analysts would expect different treatments from a vendor. A celebrity may not be interested in background information, but is only interested in the customer benefits of a product – and the money he can earn with an endorsement. He has experienced and appreciated the product and may say so in public. Often enough, though, it may be sufficient to have a celebrity appear in public with a certain product to have their fans want one as well. He may not even need to say anything. A vendor would therefore be interested in giving products away to celebrities – and exactly that is often enough done at major events like film festivals or other popular events that are closely watched by the media.

The analysts, on the other hand, cannot be bribed as easily. Actually, you do not want to bribe them at all. You want to convince them so that they can come to the conclusion themselves that they can recommend your product in good faith.

So, we see that not all influencers can be treated in the same way. And still there is a gray area between different types of influencers. In several industries and in particular in several countries public opinions are influenced significantly by academics like e.g. heads of popular research institutions or university professors. Some of them actually position themselves similarly to industry analysts. They position their research similar to the work done in industry analyst firms. It is very tempting to include these individuals into industry analyst programs.

In selected cases this approach may be justified. In general, however, this approach cannot be recommended. The main reason is again handling the confidentiality of the information you provide to the audience in your industry analyst relations program. Experience has shown that the likelihood of information leaks increases significantly as soon as you broaden the scope of your industry analyst relations program.

We are not saying that vendors should not work with universities. If their business justifies it and if they can define clear objectives, they indeed should. But they should not include professors and other leading staff into an industry analyst relations program. Instead, a vendor may want to run a special program for the educational market in general, or he may want to cooperate with specific institutions in well defined projects.

### Industry analysts and financial analysts

We know that industry analysts and financial analysts complement each other – the former focusing on products, services and solutions, the latter focusing on the financial aspects of a company.

However, the situation is not as well defined as it seems.

Industry analysts are supposed to consult with their clients on major purchasing decisions. In order to be able to do so, they obviously need a good understanding of the capabilities of different technologies. In addition, however, they also need some understanding of the financial situation of vendors. This information is needed to understand if a vendor will be around tomorrow to enhance and support the purchased equipment. The protection of an investment is dependent on the financial stability of the respective vendor.

It is needless to say that the interest in this kind of information makes industry analysts and financial analysts allies – even though they need that information for different reasons and for different clients. Financial analysts want to secure investments in stocks and venture capital. Industry analysts want to secure investments in products and services from a vendor.

Industry analysts benefit from the knowledge of financial analyst providing information on a company's financial situation and outlook. Financial analysts benefit from the knowledge of industry analysts on market share data, shipment numbers and the soundness of technologies.

Even though this should suggest that the respective roles of both these analyst groups should be well defined, reality shows that in some cases job descriptions of analysts from both communities are actually very close.

In fact they can be so close that analysts changing jobs may even change their profile, e.g. become a financial analyst, having been an industry analyst before. This is more likely for industry analysts who have been focusing on certain vertical markets rather than on specific technologies.

Some companies have drawn the conclusion that it would make sense to offer briefing sessions or analyst events (similar to press conferences) inviting a mixed audience of industry analysts and financial analysts. Having attended such events we believe it is fair to say that they should be avoided if possible. Mixing audiences in general is not a good idea. Typically one of the groups in the audience loses out while another one benefits from the event. The same is true in this case. Industry analysts and financial analysts should not be addressed with the same program. They should be approached separately and the content and messages should be tailored to their respective needs.

Having said that we should mention that one could still consider to include a very small group of financial analysts into an industry analyst program, but only on a special tiering level providing them only with a subset of the services delivered by the program. You may not want to mix them with industry analysts at events or briefings. But you may want to share newsletters or other material (like e.g. press releases) with them as appropriate.

### Conclusion

We have seen that analysts fulfill very different tasks. They can address specific markets only, they may be "number crunchers" or strategists, they may be researchers or technologists – or a mix of any of the above.

Depending on their job descriptions they tend to have different objectives and different measurement criteria and therefore would demand different services from an industry analyst program. The owner of such a program will have to pay attention to this heterogeneous audience.

We have also become aware of potential issues that could arise from the fact that we open an industry analyst program to a bigger audience. The key learning should actually be to limit the program as much as possible: Less is more.

As soon as an audience becomes too heterogeneous you will have to compromise on the message. This will result in not meeting the expectation of anybody in the audience. This may also lead to diluting the messages in a way that the true company messages are no longer coming across clearly.

An analyst program addressing a large audience may look very effective in the eyes of the vendor who wants to communicate. However, it could indeed be counterproductive since the individual analyst may get less out of the program. A program that is addressing lesser individuals, however, can be better tailored to the needs of those individuals. The likelihood of the individual analyst getting exactly the information he needs is much higher than being part of a faceless audience.

Along the same lines, industry analysts should not be attending the same events as e.g. journalists, financial analysts or customers. Only a very small number of reasons would justify an approach inviting multiple audiences to the same event.

# Chapter 4:

## The industry analyst relations program

In this chapter we want to provide as much information as possible to enable the reader to plan and execute their own industry analyst relations program. In this introduction we will assume that the reader is familiar with basic processes in PR. we will take media relations as a starting point for a journey towards industry analyst relations – knowing that journalists and analysts have different needs. But identifying and addresses these different needs will be part of the journey.

We know several standard communication processes to reach out to the media. They include distribution of PR material, e.g. via email. They also include interviews as well as press conferences. We may also want to include creative PR campaigns here, e.g. taking advantage of sponsorships, working with celebrities in consumer PR or other activities.

In a similar way we can communicate to industry analysts. However, there are some significant differences.

We would like to address three basic communication tools: general distribution, one-on-one briefings and analyst conferences.

"Hyped" activities like conferences with celebrities are not necessarily appreciated by analysts. The majority of the analysts would consider such activities as wasted time, since the news value is typically very limited. There are a few exceptions, though. Two examples for that:

A company runs a hospitality program in motor sports, since they sponsor one of the teams. The sponsorship, however, is not just based on a financial contribution to the team, but it is based on a technology partnership. In that case a visit to the race track can well be positioned as a presentation of a customer case study. we have seen analysts participating in such a program. They obviously enjoyed the racing weekend, but they appreciated even more to see how IT equipment was actually used by the teams. The experience may allow them to translate what they have seen to their customers' environments.

Celebrities become interesting to analysts as soon as they actually use the IT equipment they promote. For example, we have seen analysts in discussions with celebrity photographers about digital photography equipment. Professional photographers are a perfect source for analysts to review the quality of imaging products.

But, we should go back to the three ways of communicating with industry analysts.

**General distribution:**

Analysts are always interested in information that may be relevant to their clients. They are certainly interested in information that is distributed to the press community like press releases, media alerts and so on. Case studies, white papers, backgrounders and similar material may be even more interesting. There are multiple ways of communicating this basic material to the analyst community. The documents could be distributed by email as they become available. They could be merged into newsletters sent on a regular basis (weekly, bi-weekly, monthly – depending on the amount of news and depending on the time criticality of the news). Or, they could be placed on a website that is dedicated to the analyst community.

In real life a mix of web based repository of information for the analyst to download from as needed and newsletter based proactive distribution may be most suitable. For example, you may want to put basic data like shipment data for "market sizers" on a protected website dedicated to industry analysts. Important product news and similar information would be sent directly though. In order to avoid an information overload and to allow the analyst to focus on selected information only, you may also have your newsletter contain abstracts only while the complete documents like press releases or backgrounders are located on a website or, even better, directly linked to from the newsletter.

It turns out that analysts seem to have a preference for a monthly newsletter that contains a three to ten line summary of a topic and a link to more detailed information. Such a newsletter has the tremendous advantage that it can be archived and referred to as needed – even when the analyst is offline. Newsletters make good reading on a flight, for example.

Feedback from industry analysts show that regular newsletters are stored for future reference while message per announcement tend to get lost – apart from the fact that they tend to fill email intrays unnecessarily und run the chance of being deleted without even being read.

**One-on-one briefings:**

At first glance one may compare an analyst briefing to a press interview. Unfortunately spokespeople make the mistake sometimes to believe that both activities are indeed identical. However, the motivation of journalists and analysts for having a meeting are not identical. Therefore, there are significant differences between them. A journalist is typically looking for a strong headline. He is after breaking news, some exclusive information or a sensation – something that will sell their magazine. An analyst, however, is after facts. He is not using journalists' techniques to get more from a spokesperson than he is actually willing to say. This does not mean, though, that an analyst will not challenge a company's spokesperson. He will do so. But he will focus just on facts.

As a result, the atmosphere in an analyst briefing is very different to that in a press interview. A briefing is much more open. It is a discussion of two equals rather than one individual driving the discussion while the second one is in the role of simply reacting to questions – unless he is an excellent spokesperson who is not just passive but able to influence the direction of an interview.

**Analyst conference:**

Vendors who are serious about industry analyst relations will not simply bring journalists and analysts together to jointly attend a press conference. They will separate the audiences and run a press conference and an analyst conference separately.

We strongly recommend not to make use of the same patterns for both events. The agendas should be designed differently to address the respective needs of the two audiences. Also, speakers may be different at both events. For example, engineers with no appropriate media training must never attend a press conference. At an analyst event those engineers – after only a brief coaching – can add a lot of value, though.

A significant difference between press conferences and analyst events is the fact that analysts should get access to presentation materials a few days before the conference. This allows them to prepare properly and to take down notes during the presentations.1

Finally we want to stress the fact that it is appropriate for an industry analyst relations manager after a major announcement to come back to the participating analysts and collect their feedback. Many analysts are very open to provide some comments2. This information should certainly go into the de-briefing material compiled after major activities (see also next chapter).

> **Case Study:**
>
> Analyst conferences are typically organised by a vendor or an organisation that is interested in passing on news to the analyst community. In some cases, they invite partners or customers to present as references or to make a story complete.
>
> A business partner may complement the news from a vendor. For example, a hardware vendor may introduce a new computer platform with an endorsement from a software vendor. In another case, a manufacturer may be supported by one of his main channel partners. Finally, customers can act as references for a new product that they have already evaluated and tested.
>
> Analysts are interested in getting a complete picture to consult their clients in a best possible manner. Thus, they appreciate such events where they get a complete overview.
>
> In this context it should be mentioned that communication agencies can contribute significantly to the success of industry analyst relations. Not only can they support their client, but they can even become the driver for multiple clients by organising a conference where they bring several clients together

[1] As a side note it should be mentioned that the presentations are preferred in PowerPoint format over any other format. If information is provided in this format, the respective communications manager or analyst relations manager needs to ensure, though, that no company internal information is left in the speaker notes in the PowerPoint file – a very common mistake.

[2] It should be noted, however, that some analysts take a different approach. They would insist on selling their feedback as consultancy to a vendor – rather than providing feedback informally and free of charge.

with a group of analysts. The format of "many-to-many-events" (rather than "one-to-many-events") is particularly interesting for smaller companies that do not have critical mass to run major events by themselves. If an agency has multiple clients in a certain industry, they can run a conference by adding companies to the agenda that complement each other, i.e. that address a complete value chain.

On a local level such events have been done in selected industries with positive results.

The above has shown that the content provided to industry analysts is different from the content provided to the press. We still want to share the same information like for example a strategy announcement or a new product introduction. But the following example illustrates the difference between what is relevant to an analyst and what is picked up by a journalist.

We assume that a company brings the fastest computer or processor of its kind in the world to market. The fact that the new product sets a new world record is certainly worth an article in the media – and it is pretty obvious what the headline might look like. If the PR department of that company packages the news appropriately, a journalist writing for an IT magazine can hardly avoid writing about the topic.

Analysts who pick up the news will also write about it in their newsletter, or they may even write a research note on it. But, we need to remember that the objective of an industry analyst relations program is to have analysts recommend a product or a solution to their clients. In order to achieve that goal a pure product announcement – even if it is about the fastest new solution in the market – will not do the trick. Analysts are in the IT industry for too long to understand that vendors are leap-frogging each other on an ongoing basis. This is a common pattern for decades. Therefore, a product that is superior today may be inferior tomorrow as soon as another vendor brings its latest product to market.

Industry analysts will certainly be interested to understand what is beyond such a "point product". They will ask questions like what solutions are available on the processor or the computer. The best computer will be useless for their clients if it does not support the software needed by them. Another question they will have is if the vendor can sustain its leadership. They will ask questions about life times, support commitments, and so on. We need to remember that industry analysts consult typically with major corporations that expect guidance from them to make the right purchase decision worth millions of dollars. Beyond the purchase price there are typically significant investments in process changes and structural changes in the company. In other words, the decision can impact the performance of the company significantly. And, in some cases a wrong decision may even have an effect on the company's existence. Such a decision will not be dependent on a vendor announcing just a powerful new product.

In this respect commercial customers behave exactly opposite to consumers. While consumers expect to have always the latest and greatest to be hip, commercial customers can easily live with much longer product life cycles. We all know the dilemma we are in with our operating system on our PC: A new one is introduced every two or three years and we will have to upgrade to it to guarantee long term support – regardless if we actually need the upgrade or not.

As we mentioned above, the vendor will have to proof that there is a scalable solution available on top of the introduced hardware, he will have to proof that he provides long-lasting appropriate services and support and he will have to proof that they have a stable financial background to provide customers a safe growth path and support for years to come.

We have seen a lot of examples in the hi-tech industry over the years of superior technologies losing out to lower performing solutions. We have seen fast computers not being endorsed by the analyst community because they questioned the future of the technology or the future of the vendor. DEC's Alpha processor, for example, was very powerful but the company had significant challenges to get it endorsed by the analyst community at the time. Most of us are probably familiar with the example of the Beta video tape technology losing to the apparently inferior VHS technology. We have seen other superior technologies not making it because of a lack of commitment from vendors, lack of marketing power (just remember the "operating system wars") or simply lack of scalability of a solution to provide a growth path to the customer.

All the above shows that we tend to focus our message to the press on only one or two main points. The message needs to be snappy. It needs to translate into a catching headline.

The message we disclose to industry analysts tends to be more complex. We can afford to be more complex. For example, we can embed our news into a complex messaging framework that provides a good understanding not only of the specific news we want to share, but also the context in which it can contribute to an end user's solution.

All of the above also shows that an industry analyst program certainly needs to go well beyond just communicating new product introductions in newsletters, briefings or analyst conferences.

**A true industry analyst relations program is not just a mechanical communications tool.**

**A true industry analyst relations program is an attitude.**

A valuable industry analyst program requires commitment from a vendor – not only from the employees working in the program, but also from higher level management and top executives, including the CEO. They are the ones who can address topics like the company's direction and strategy. They are the ones who can generate trust in a company, because they are the ones who make the respective decisions. And – at the same time – they are the ones who benefit most from the relationships with industry analysts.

One industry analyst was very straightforward recently, when he was asked what individual representing a vendor he would like to talk to. Ideally they want to talk to the person who is actually accountable for what they presents. This could be the CEO, for corporate strategies, or an R&D manager for product developments.

**Spokespeople**

The above leads us naturally to a discussion about our company's spokespeople. Without spokespeople there is no industry analyst relations program!

You may argue that you can still run an industry analyst relations program that is simply built on compiling a regular newsletter with content taken from the PR department, business intelligence and other company resources. This newsletter would then be sent out to a defined distribution list containing all analysts addressed by the program.

You can obviously run such a process. But please, do not call it an industry analyst relations program! It is hardly a program nor does it take into account the "relations" factor. Good speakers are needed to get the messages across properly. Good relationships between company executives and industry analysts are the foundation of a successful program.

Since the communication with analysts is less formal than that with media representatives one can include a broader spectrum of speakers into an analyst relations program.

Just like in a good PR program it helps tremendously to put a roster of speakers together per topic. The topics are obviously defined by the messages that a company is interested to deliver to the public and by the objectives defined for the industry analyst program. Last, but not least, the topics are defined by the analysts' fields of interest. It should be stressed that spokespeople should not only be defined for proactively communicated topics, but also for reactive responses to anticipated questions and topic areas.

Both analysts and vendor spokespeople are embedded into their respective company's objectives, mission statements and focus areas. The following diagram provides an overview.

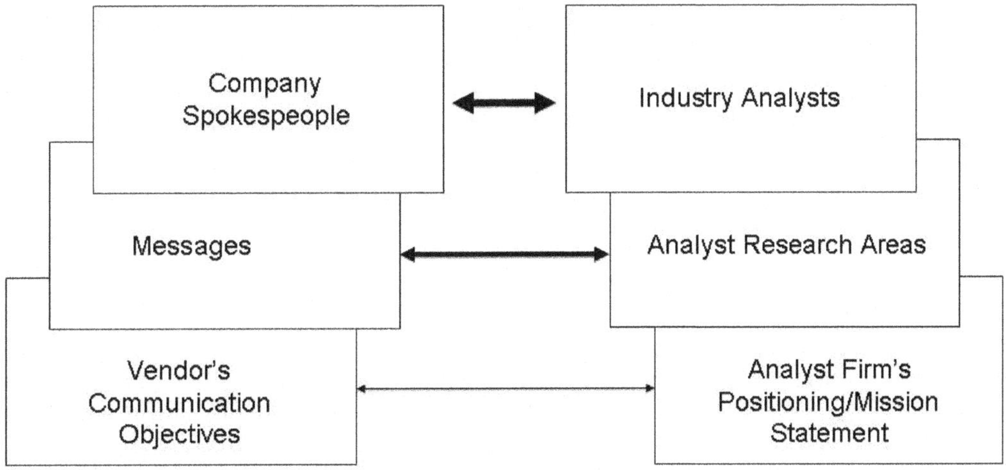


Figure 4.1: Spokespeople - analysts

The basis for a cooperation between a vendor and an analyst firm is the fact that they both address the same market. An analyst firm defines their value add typically very well. They identify their target audience well and they position their services well. A vendor typically defines communication objectives related to its business. The demand for an industry analyst relations program is derived from these objectives. They obviously go along with the positioning of the analyst firms they select for co-operation.

A messaging framework is built by a vendor on top of its communication objectives. These messages address a specific value or a specific portfolio the vendor provides to the market. It corresponds to the research areas of individual analysts. For example, if a vendor wants to focus on a specific market segment like a defined vertical market, they may be interested in working with the respective analyst who addresses that segment – rather than with an analyst who addresses a certain technology.

Finally, the messages define the spokesperson or spokespersons who address a specific analyst. It needs to be noted that this argument also needs to be turned around: An analyst's objectives and focus areas define the spokesperson they want to talk to.

If the ground work has been done properly, then two people will meet who not only speak the same language, but who should be interested to exchange information and to learn from each other.

We have mentioned earlier that a vendor can be more flexible with the selection of spokespeople than they can be in a PR program. Analysts may have very different needs and vendors can address them openly (within certain guidelines defined by corporate policies) with senior executive staff all the way to R&D engineers who are educated on basic communication principles. Experience shows that openness with analysts pays back. Trying to hide information artificially is neither in the interest of the analysts nor can it be in the interest of the vendor – unless a very special situation demands to withhold information from the analyst community. Being protective with information for example also means that analysts will not be able to reflect on them. They will not be able to provide initial confidential feedback to the vendor allowing the vendor to do corrective moves before public announcements, for example.

Representatives from the following departments should be considered as spokespeople to work with industry analysts:

A company's CEO must show commitment to dedicating time to industry analysts. They can speak on behalf of the entire company. they can discuss strategic moves and general directions. It is their task to ensure confidence in the future of the company. Louis Columbus[1] has dedicated an entire chapter in his book on the impact of a CEO. we have no intention to repeat his comments. Still, we fully support his view and want to stress that analysts indeed pay a lot of attention to the attitude of a company's CEO. A passionate CEO gives them the confidence that the company is indeed committed to what they are doing and that they are hungry for business. Turning the argument around, a CEO who is invisible to them or showing the wrong attitude can have a very negative impact opinions formed about the company and on the relationships with industry analysts in general.

Product managers are the perfect counterparts for analysts who focus on certain technologies. They are interested in the product strategy, the product positioning and all the technical details.

Analysts who focus on sizing the markets are interested in receiving shipment and pricing data from vendors. Contacts to provide that kind of data reside in a planning or even in a financial department.

Sales or business management is a preferred audience industry analysts want to talk to because they are close to the customer. With them they can verify trends they observe in the industry on a micro scale.

Finally, analysts appreciate to get access to technical engineers, either working in the field with customers or working in R&D departments (see below case study). Field engineers are maybe more a target for consultants. But R&D engineers are certainly a good audience for analysts to spend time with as appropriate. we have seen technologies where the request from analysts was clearly articulated to have access to R&D engineers from time to time. we have seen other technology areas where the demand was significantly lower. Vendors need to make a decision based on the market they are in, their interest in confidentiality and also based on the communication skills of their engineers...

Marketing: we think it is fair to say that members from a marketing department are least in demand by industry analysts. Marketing professionals are often seen as a filter for information rather than a valuable resource. Marketing managers may be the hosts of analyst conferences, though, coordinating the overall communication and performance.

---

[1] Getting Results From Your Analyst Relations Strategies, Louis Columbus, LWC Research

**Case study:**

Talking about spokespeople: The company Hewlett-Packard runs an annual event for journalists as well as industry analysts in Europe called the HP Lab University. For two reasons this event is a good example for successful industry analyst relations. Despite our earlier comments that mixed audiences should be avoided if possible, the event is successful addressing press and analysts at the same time. Secondly, in the context of talking about spokespeople it must be mentioned that speakers at this event are predominantly R&D engineers and managers.

Objective of the event is to present news across a wide product portfolio. The event runs for several days. Several sessions run in parallel, and they are repeated several times. All participants can create their own personalized agenda depending on their own individual areas of interest. The number of participants per session is kept low to allow for interaction between speakers and participants. Analysts and journalists share the same sessions to learn about and experience new and upcoming technologies. One session, however, is for analysts only, giving the organizers the opportunity to address topics that are not relevant or not intended for the press.

The format of this event requires a lot of planning and in particular coaching of the speakers. Not only do they need to be trained to communicate to press and analysts, but also do they need to be able to differentiate between their respective needs. The efforts are justified looking at the results of the event. Industry analysts appreciate the event, since they get a complete overview at a single event, rather than attending multiple briefings. And, they have the option to discuss details with the experts to collect the information they require to consult with their clients. And finally, they receive strategic information and tactical product news at a single event.

**Do's and dont's for spokespeople**

The best industry analyst program can only be successful with good spokespeople. There are several levels of trainings available for speakers from generic presentation trainings to individual coaching.

The following is the briefest of all guidelines for spokespeople who are supposed to present to industry analysts. Consider it to be the yeast of all trainings.

**Do's:**
Before a briefing:
Communicate to the industry analyst relations team that you meet analysts!
Know your content!
Know your competition!
Do a dry run!

**During a briefing:**
Be honest, natural and open!
Encourage interaction!

**After a briefing:**
Provide feedback to the industry analyst relations team!

**Dont's:**
Don't sell! (Avoid marketing hype!)
Avoid bashing the competition!
Don't preach!
Don't call an analyst 'consultant'!
Don't quote analysts to other analysts!
Don't brief analysts for more than 1.5 to 2 hours!
Don't plainly contradict analysts (and their ego)!

But how about the industry analyst relations professionals? Is their role to manage the communication with industry analysts – or do they operate as spokespeople themselves?

The answer depends on the size of a company, and therefore on the size of the analyst relations program. And it depends on who actually runs the program. we believe, for example, that it is not appropriate to outsource the industry analyst relations program simply as part of the PR activities and then have PR agency staff representing a company as spokespeople. They should indeed focus on managing the communication rather than communicating themselves. An exception could be senior contracted specialists who are focusing on industry analyst relations rather than being "diverted" PR professionals. In other words: Agencies with a dedicated analyst relations practice should have an advantage over agencies that address analyst relations with standard PR staff.

In-house staff should indeed be skilled to represent the company – or at least cover selected topics – as a spokesperson. It would not be appropriate for them to arrange a 1:1 with a company spokesperson for any query an analyst may have. They should be able to judge if a briefing with a higher level executive is needed or if they can address the topic themselves right away. Criteria to make such a decision would be tiring level of the analyst, time to respond to an analyst query and importance and sensitivity of the topic.

All spokespeople included in an industry analyst relations program should be defined way ahead of being needed in a specific project like a briefing or a conference. They should be tagged with defined topics and potentially with a specific audience. For example, a company may want to run a "buddy program" where selected executives are defined as primary "go-to persons" for selected top industry analysts.

It is recommended to put a spokespeople matrix together for the company that may look like the following:

| Speaker | Topic | Audience | Remarks |
|---|---|---|---|
| Tom Thompson | Corporate Strategy | Tier 1 only | |
| Dave Davison | Corporate Strategy | All analysts | Backup for Tom |
| Paul Paulson | UK Business | UK analysts only | |
| Peter Petersen | Shipment/Pricing | All | |
| John Johnson | Products | All | "Buddy" for Joe Smith/GHI |
| Mary Merrill | Automotive Industry | Only firms ABC and DEF | "Buddy" for Carla Speed |
| James Jameson | Emerging Technologies | Only firm GHI | For firm JKL only with formal NDA! |

Figure 4.2: Spokespeople list

The above diagram may require some explanation:

Tom Thompson may be the company's CEO. His time is limited. He is made available to top tier analysts only.

The company seems to have made a bad experience with the analyst firm JKL. It specifically requests a formal non-disclosure agreement to be signed by the firm before they receive information on emerging technologies. Maybe JKL has violated an informal agreement earlier.

Two spokespeople are dedicated counterparts ("buddies") for selected analysts. They should consolidate company information and act as an interface to the selected analysts.

Paul Paulson may be a local UK business manager. He is supposed to interact with analysts with UK responsibility only. Since the experience in the UK may be different from international trends they may mislead analysts with international responsibility. Therefore, they should be exposed to analysts with UK responsibility only.

### Spokespeople guidelines

Every company has its own guidelines and policies as to what can be said in public and what is company confidential information. In addition, companies listed at the stock exchange need to follow additional rules related to so-called blackout periods (or: quiet periods), i.e. the time before an earnings announcement.

You can split the information that can be shared into four groups:

1. Information already announced:
   Since the information is already in the public domain, it is obvious that a spokesperson can talk about it in meetings with industry analysts. In this category falls information such as:
   - Company brochures
   - Previous earnings announcements
   - Annual reports
   - News releases (incl. facts and opinions articulated in them)
   - Data sheets
2. Information on introduced products:
   Again, the products were introduced already. Thus, most companies allow their spokespeople to address topics like these:
   - Product (or service) specifications
   - Market positioning
   - Product features and benefits
   - Available solutions (partner solutions included if agreed with the company's business partner, e.g. an application provider)
   - Customer references (if agreed with the customer)
   - Prices (a detailed pricing structure including margins can typically NOT be disclosed)
3. Product strategy and positioning:
   The list of items in this category depends significantly on a company's policies and on the state of their product rollout. An overview of the current product families and the overall offering can be done. Discussing and highlighting the company's strategic focus areas is typically also appropriate. Projections into the future, however, can often not be disclosed. Especially it would be inappropriate to pre-announce upcoming news.
4. Corporate policies and practices:
   Again, in this category we look at topics that may or may not be disclosed, depending on corporate policies. Typical items in this group include:
   - Corporate objectives
   - Environmental plans

- Employee profit share schemes and stock plans
- Other employee related topics like a workforce reduction plan or an early retirement program

Information that cannot be talked about includes the following:

1. Financial projections (revenue, profits, orders, quotas, shipments, ...)
2. Some companies have clear guidelines to what level the results of individual entities of the company can be broken down to.
3. Marketing strategy: Some data like for example advertising plans may be subject to public disclosure (depending on objectives and corporate policies), some other data like sales force deployment may not be to avoid aiding the competition.
4. Competitive remarks:
    - Do not disparage competitors' products!
    - Do not disparage competitors' strategies!
5. It may be inappropriate to comment on market share data. A spokesperson may not want to confirm neither comment of the accuracy of an analyst's figures.
6. It is certainly inappropriate to discuss analyst data with analysts from other firms or in front of a mixed analyst audience.
7. Disclosing information about the relationship with business partners (OEMs, VABs, channel partners, suppliers, etc) and customers is always subject to approval by the respective company.
8. Products under development
9. Negotiations underway
10. Legal matters, including:
    - Patent infringements
    - Law suits, pending cases
    - Negotiations
    - Tax matters

**Message consistency**

The following remarks may be self-explanatory to some readers. To some others they may trigger some action items.

It may sound obvious that all outbound communication from a company is consistent. Still, many corporations do not follow this simple guideline. we are sure we all know examples of inconsistent communication – not from our own company of course, but from observations in the industry or just from following the daily news on TV. We have probably seen cases like one spokesperson of a company confirming some rumors to a journalist while another one denies them. These contradictions are obvious. Sometimes, however, they are more hidden.

Just assume examples like the following:

A marketing manager predicts a significant market growth that the company will benefit from. In an interview with an SCM[1] magazine, the company's supply chain manager discusses the fact that the company is not planning to increase its production capacities. These two public statements do not seem to go together and will certainly cause confusion.

The business manager of a company's consumer products department announces a strong focus of the company on the consumer market with significant investments. The manager of the business-to-business department makes similar statements about the business. None of them mentions the respective other spokesperson. The result is again confusion since the strategic direction of the company is unclear.

One company spokesperson describes the company strategy to reside on three pillars: hardware, software and services being closely interconnected. Another speaker does not even mention services. So, is the company really committed to services?

These simple examples indicate that all outbound communication must be based on an agreed messaging framework. This framework should then be the basis for all outbound communication. It secures consistent messaging across different target audiences. It also secures consistent messaging to one target audience, e.g. from different departments of the company or from one department over time.

We stress the importance of consistency here, since analysts typically try to establish multiple entries into a company. They will take advantage of that and will check their sources for consistency.

European analysts working for international analyst firms may get invitations to European and to worldwide analyst conferences. They would listen to European and to worldwide spokespeople, e.g. from North America. It should be expected that they would not hear contradicting news from these two sources. In fact, analysts may even focus more on what they do not hear rather than what they do hear. This approach makes it even more important to follow a strict messaging framework, since the services business from the third example above may have a significant issue after it has been ignored accidentally in a keynote presentation.

### Analyst tiering

The term "analyst tiering" has been mentioned a few times already. We now want to explain in detail what is actually meant by it. In simple terms, tiering analysts is prioritizing them. The prioritized order, though, would be dependent on the criteria we apply. It is therefore relevant to have a closer look at the criteria we want to make use of. In addition we need to define the service levels we provide to the analysts per tiering level.

A common mistake of new analyst relations managers is to offer identical services to all analysts they work with. As long as the number of analysts is small, this ap-

[1] SCM: supply chain management

proach may work. As soon as the program grows, though, the limited resources may prohibit to continue with this approach. But there is an even more serious reason that speaks against serving all analysts the same. In chapter 7 we will see that we need to prioritize analysts to meet our objectives. In particular, we have to focus to ensure an appropriate return on the investment we put into the program.

The value of individual industry analysts and of analyst firms will be defined differently depending on who in an organization is asked to provide input. The planning and forecasting team will favor analysts who focus on market sizing and demand prediction. The sales team will favor analysts who can share customer insights. And the marketing team may favor analysts who can be invited as charismatic guest speakers at company events. None of these criteria must be considered when tiering industry analysts.

The single measure that must be considered is the influence of the analyst on the customer community that is addressed by the vendor who runs the analyst relations program. In other words, the sales impact is what counts.

Influence is the impact an analyst or an analyst firm has on buying decisions. It must not be mixed up with visibility! For example, quotes in the press certainly count as visibility. They only count as influence if the quotes are directly related to topics that have an impact on buying decision. When Scott McNealy announced in April of 2006 that he will step down as CEO of Sun Microsystems, the comments of one single industry analyst were quoted in the press more than all others combined. This analyst had been known for following Sun very closely and it was obvious that he would be a good source for a statement on McNealy's departure. It is more than questionable, though, if these generic quotes contributed significantly to customers' purchase decisions.

It is more important to analyze the customer base of an analyst or an analyst firm and derive a value from that analysis that represents the "controlled" purchase volume of that analyst or that firm. It will turn out that in most markets the 80/20 rule is valid, i.e. no more than 20 per cent of the analysts influence 80 per cent of the available spending money. Those 20 per cent (or even less) of the analysts are moved into the tier 1 category.

The remaining 80 to 90 per cent of the analysts must be split again into two levels. The vast majority of them will end up in the tier 3 level. However, a few of them – probably again around 20 to 30 per cent of all analysts – are in a special position. They may not be very influential directly with customers. But they are in a close network with other analysts and thus influence significantly within the analyst community. In order to understand these interdependencies it is crucial that an analyst relations manager understands the analyst's respective networks. Bigger analyst firms, for example, sometimes subcontract to smaller ones. Or, there are relationships between analysts that are purely on an informal basis.

To summarize, it is recommended to split the analyst community into 3 tiering levels per this scheme:

**Tier 1:** Only analysts with a significant direct impact on purchase decisions (10 to 20 per cent of all analysts).

**Tier 2:** Analysts with a good network (20 to 30 per cent of all analysts).

**Tier 3:** All others (50 to 70 per cent of all analysts).

This structure allows to prioritize the target audience. If the resources available for industry analyst relations are only small, then it may make sense to offer services to tier 1 analysts only. It is easily possible to focus an analyst relations program on only three firms. The number of addressed analysts is not necessarily a crucial parameter in analyst relations. A focused program may be more effective than a "high and wide" program serving any analyst requesting support.

Services provided per tiering level again depend on the resources available for the analyst relations program. An option may be the following approach:

**Tier 1:** Dedicated one-on-one briefings are provided. Access to selected high level executives is available.

**Tier 2:** Analysts are invited to group briefings.

**Tier 3:** No invitations to any briefings. Information is distributed through a website or newsletters only.

This can only be a recommendation, of course. The details will always depend on the respective industry a company is operating in and on the available resources.

To wrap this chapter up we want to articulate one more aspect of tiering. We can expect the top tier analysts to be senior individuals. We can get their attention by offering them a special treatment making no secret of the fact that it is offered to handpicked individuals only. For example, we may want to invite them to an event that is for team leaders of major analyst houses only. We want to make the invitation non-transferable. It would then be counter productive if the invited analyst meets second tier colleagues at that event. And it would be even worse, if the line between analysts and other influencers has not been drawn carefully in the first place (see chapter 3),e.g. senior analysts run into participants at the event they would not have expected there. Not only would they feel they have been misguided with the invitation and the real intention of the organizers, but also could feel personally misplaced or even downgraded. Tiering is one way of avoiding such conflicts with analysts' egos.

## Chapter 5:

## Archives and Infrastructure Tools

In this section we want to have a look at the infrastructure you want to have available when starting an industry analyst relations program.

You want basic information about your analyst audience. You also want to track your past and ongoing communication with the analyst community, in particular you want to maintain a history of the individual analysts and the information exchanged with them. In addition, you want to have a database with contact details of the analysts you selected for your program.

### Analyst briefing documentation

An industry analyst briefing should be well documented for several reasons. We want to ensure that all company internal stakeholders in the briefing are well informed in a consistent way. We want to ensure that all involved individuals understand their role and the common objectives. We want to ensure that we capture the analysts' feedback. And finally we want to ensure that we learn from the exercise.

We want to discuss three documents in this sub-chapter that we complete per briefing. In the early phase we want to compile a briefing plan that is the basis for all stakeholders who need to buy into the project. We then have to prepare all individuals who are actively involved in the event. This is typically done with a briefing document. After the event we want to document everything that we may need for future reference. All documentation should be archived for future use as needed, for example in one of the tools we will describe later in this chapter.

#### Briefing plan

The briefing plan is typically written well in advance of the briefing itself. Exact timing depends on the speed of the industry your business is in and on the size of your company. Since more stakeholders are typically involved in larger enterprises, it is recommended to allow for more planning time the bigger a company is.

The briefing plan is not a standalone document. It obviously needs to be fully aligned with the overall marketing and communication plans of the company. In particular, it needs to be aligned with the overall industry analyst relations plan, if such a plan exists separately. An individual briefing would not necessarily be listed in an overall generic plan, which may be valid for an entire year. An individual briefing is the tactical implementation of the strategic plan supporting its goals and objectives.

A briefing plan should consist of the following parts:

- Executive summary
- Business objectives (taken from overall plan)

- Marketing/communication objectives
- Industry analyst relations objectives
- Situation analysis (potentially including SWOT1 analysis)
- Key messages for the analysts
- Proposed spokespeople
- Audience definition
- Participating analysts' biographies and/or profiles
- Metrics
- Proposal for future activities building on the briefing.

All of the above is for approval by decision makers and stakeholders in the project. It is also the framework for additional tactical information like timing, location, agenda proposal, roles and responsibilities details, budget, etc.

We would like to highlight the line item 'metrics' above. It should be emphasized that the results of the project must be measurable – otherwise the briefing should be questioned, since there would be no goal and no accountability. Defined goals must be in line with overall communication objectives, they must be realistic and they must be relevant.

Briefing[2] document for participants

The briefing document is intended for spokespeople and other company representatives attending the analyst briefing. It should contain a summary of the above briefing plan. In addition it needs to contain additional information to prepare spokespeople for the event and the logistical details.

In particular, the company spokespeople need to get an update on the analysts they are going to meet. The biographies and the profiles discussed in the next subchapter should therefore be included in the briefing document. A summary of the recent events the analysts attended and a list of other company speakers the analysts met recently needs to be included. Also, their recent comments revealing their attitudes and public statements need to be in the document.

The briefing document ensures that a spokesperson is aware of potential issues the company may have with analysts. Maybe an analyst has recently questioned the quality of the company's products or they have questioned the business strategy. The briefing document ensures that a speaker does not run into an open knife. Foreseeable issues must not come as a surprise to them during a briefing session.

As a reminder, existing company drawer statements addressing specific topics should also be included in the briefing document.

---

[1] For SWOT analysis see also the next chapter.

[2] "Briefing" in this context refers to briefing the internal stakeholders on the intended event. It does not refer to the analyst briefing itself in this case.

Finally, the document contains all necessary logistics depending on the speakers' expectation. This may include transfers to and from the event venue, individual time tables, contact details of the attending analyst relations staff etc.

De-briefing/summary document

The basis for the de-briefing or summary document is again the initial briefing plan. The summary is written for multiple purposes. First of all we want to capture everything we have learned during the briefing. We document the analysts' response to the briefing. Positive comments – and more importantly reserved or negative comments – need to be documented. It is important not only to document formal analyst feedback, but also informal comments or remarks. They can be very revealing. Not only may you get unexpected questions, but you may also get indications on competitive moves the analysts are already aware of.

The analysts' reaction to your briefing may result in immediate or future actions. They could range from providing more detailed information or background information on the topics discussed in the briefing all the way to considering a special program for selected analysts.

The de-briefing document should also include a summary of the output generated by the briefed analysts. These could be immediate so-called "first takes", i.e. quick information for their clients together with a preliminary judgment of the analyst. These could also include detailed research notes. And, last but not least, you need to capture press references, i.e. comments the analysts made in press articles.

Most importantly, a de-briefing document needs to show if the goals defined in the initial plan were met or not.

All these items should allow to include proposals for next steps in the industry analyst program. Like every communication program, the industry analyst relations program develops in circles. The evaluation of one project should feed into the situation analysis for the next project.

**Biography and Profile**

It is highly recommended to build up an archive containing all relevant information on the analysts that are included in an industry analyst relations program. Key documents in this database are analyst biographies and analyst profiles.

An analyst's biography as provided for example on www.analystprofiles.com or on many analyst firms' websites contains at least two topics:

A personal biography

This biography contains the analyst's current job title including ideally a brief description of their role. It also contains a brief history of their previous jobs that allows to gain some understanding of the person's experience.

Ideally the biography is accompanied by a recent photo of the analyst. This can turn out to be most valuable when meeting the analyst for the first time and identifying them in a larger crowd, e.g. at a trade show.

Research focus

This information is key. In order to avoid bombarding the analyst with information that is not useful for them, an analyst relations program must target information to individual analysts per their specific focus areas. If information is distributed generically to a larger audience without paying attention to respective needs, then analysts tend to ignore the information. Most of them would even be annoyed. There is a high likelihood that all your communication to them will be automatically re-directed to the waste basket in the future – including that information that was really relevant for them…

The research focus can address multiple aspects of the person's role. It typically specifies the technologies an analyst is specialized in. It may also specify the kind of client the analyst is addressing (e.g. end users vs. vendors, or enterprises vs. small/ medium business, or specific vertical industries).

The above information is basic. It is highly recommended, however, to have even more information available about the analysts. For example, when working with analysts for some time it is almost unavoidable to learn about the person's private background like for example their hobbies. Such information may be very useful to have. For example, if a vendor runs a hospitality program on top of some sponsorships, it may or may not be appropriate to invite an analyst to participate in one of its events depending on their personal preferences. Or, if you know that an analyst is allergic to fish then it is inappropriate to invite them to a seafood restaurant. Access to this kind of information may be very useful indeed. Storage of such information is subject to local privacy regulations, however. It is highly recommended for an analyst relations professional to make themself familiar with such regulations and with corporate policies that may be interfering as well.

It is highly recommended to have two versions of an analyst's biography or profile on file. The first one contains all details as described above. The second one is a short version that can be used e.g. for company internal spokespeople briefings. For example, it is a good practice to compile a briefing book for executives before an analyst briefing (see above). In this document executives will find a management summary of all information needed to prepare for a conference or an analyst briefing. These briefing documents can be compiled very quickly if short profiles are maintained on an ongoing basis – and sometimes they have to be put together very quickly because often enough the lead time to an event is only very short.

**Analyst firms' profiles**

Just like the individual analyst is profiled, the analyst firms should be profiled as well. Typically a paragraph or two may be sufficient. The profile may contain generic information like the company's focus areas and their outreach. It should also contain information that is specifically relevant to the vendor that runs the analyst relations program.

Specific information may be information on joint customers. It may be the importance or relevancy the analyst firm has for the vendor. It should also list if the vendor is a client of the analyst firm to understand the relevance the analyst firm has for the company or for individual branches of the company.

### Contact details

One may argue that a telephone number and an email address are sufficient to have nowadays.

We would recommend to collect some more information if ever possible.

But before we continue we need to add a disclaimer at this point: An analyst relations person must be aware of the analyst firm's policies to contact analysts! Some firms allow access to analysts directly without any issues – some others are very protective and allow access to their analysts only via a well defined and communicated process. (A good relationship with the individual analysts sometimes allows to bypass that process. It is strongly recommended to do so only, however, when explicitly agreed with the respective analyst.)

Now back to the contact details an analyst relations manager should have access to. For example, you may want to have multiple telephone numbers on file including the analyst's direct office number, the switchboard number and their mobile phone number. This would enable an analyst relations manager to get access to the analyst at an instant if breaking news needs to be communicated in a very short timeframe.

Most valuable, by the way, is to have contact details also of the analyst's administrative assistant.

Additional information that should be available includes the analysts' postal addresses and their FAX number (yes, they are still in use sometimes).

It is important to know precisely where an analyst physically resides. It turns out that many vendors do make a generic assumption that all analysts of a firm are based in their main office. This results in embarrassing situations.

According to anecdotes shared by analysts, it must have happened more than once that an analyst based in London, UK, was invited by a vendor's executive for dinner because he "happens to be in town". It only turned out later that he had referred to Boston, Massachusetts (the analyst firm's headquarters), not knowing that the respective analyst was based on a different continent in a different time zone...

### Communication and history tracking

In order to understand an analyst's information level and in order to be consistent with previous activities and messages, an analyst relations manager must track all contacts made with an analyst.

The history should list all the recent vendor's activities an analyst has participated in. This may have been dedicated briefings, industry analyst conferences, press events, attendance at activities at trade shows or other events. The history should also list one-on-one meetings of company representatives and the analyst. The record should name the person the analyst has met and the topic discussed.

Such a list reveals immediately if an analyst has been kept up to date or if a speaker in an upcoming briefing needs to go back a bit to bring the analyst up to date. The list also reveals if an analyst has been regularly invited to annual events – and thus should be invited again next time to be consistent (unless a conscious decision is made against it).

The history should also highlight potential past and current issues with the analyst. For example, he may not connect well with certain executives (but very well with others), he may have commented negatively on products or strategies, or he may be known for strongly endorsing a competitor's solution. This is again important briefing material for spokespeople who are supposed to meet that particular industry analyst.

**Access to research**

Last but not least the owner of an industry analyst relations program needs to have access to the analysts' output. This is not a given since it involves costs. Since research is typically purchased by the company's business intelligence department a close cooperation with the industry analyst relations program is needed.

Companies that decide to outsource their industry analyst relations program to an agency need to pay attention to the fact that the agency has formal access to research. we stress the term "formal" here, since for example access to material based on good personal relationships is not only insufficient, since it does not secure access to all material, but it also is insecure since the departure of a single agency employee may cut the good connection. It is strongly recommended to explicitly spell out the need to that access in an RFP ("request for proposal") to an agency. It is mandatory not only for the daily work, it is also a must have for the evaluation of the effectiveness of an industry analyst relations program.

Especially smaller or local PR agencies that are asked to manage an industry analyst relations program in addition to the PR program are typically challenged with that request since the cost to get access to research material may be prohibitive for them. Larger international agencies or dedicated AR agencies can justify the expenses since they can distribute the cost across a larger number of clients.

## Chapter 6:

## The Industry Analyst Relations Program Plan

By now we should have a good basis for creating a first industry analyst relations plan for our organization. In this chapter we will discuss the content that should be covered by a complete plan. we want to stress that this plan is not going to cover tactical activities like for example an analyst briefing. We have looked into such a plan already in the previous chapter.

We now want to develop a strategic plan that is going through a major revision only every year or so. This plan needs to be consistent with other functional plans like the advertising plan or the PR plan. Again, as stated several times before, coordination across the entire communication mix is fundamental. Also, the industry analyst relations program plan must be embedded into the marketing plan and it must comply with and support the overall business plan.

Every plan must contain four fundamental parts:

- Situation analysis
- Objectives
- Implementation description
- Metrics

We will touch on all four aspects in detail.

### Situation analysis

In the situation analysis we want to ensure that all company internal stakeholders have a common understanding of the status quo. We want to list the analysts that have been identified so far and that we are working with already. A review of the recent activities is helpful as well as a summary of the current attitudes of the analysts.

Ideally a metrics has been in place already for some time. In that case the most recent results must be listed in this first part of the plan.

One of the best methods to describe the current situation is a SWOT analysis. SWOT stands for Strength/Weakness/Opportunity/Threats. Basically, this method is a very straightforward documentation of all items that contribute to the current status of the company's industry analyst relations program.

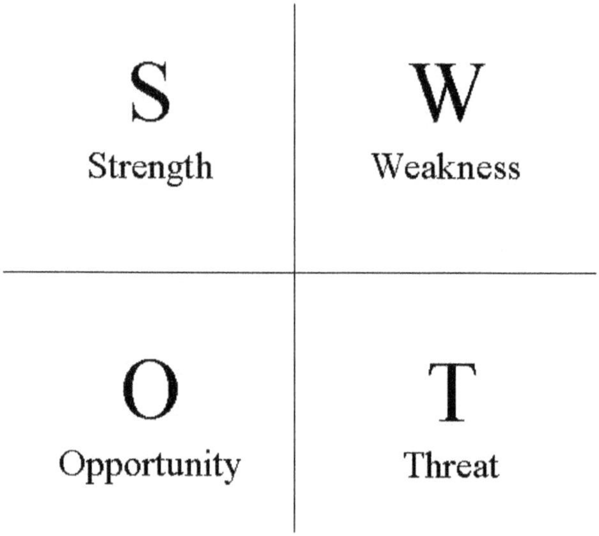


**Figure 6.1:** SWOT analysis

In the "Strength" section we list all facts that allow us to win in the market. Typical examples include superior products, strong brand recognition, complete solutions portfolio, excellent partnerships with complementing vendors, high market shares or price/performance leadership. We should not only look at our product offerings here, though. Other facts like a loyal indirect channel, an excellent sales force, financial stability of the company or others can contribute significantly to the company's strength. Finally, we must add existing good relationships with analysts and analyst firms here.

In the "Weakness" section we list facts that may allow our competitors to score against our company. Typical examples include high prices, inferior products or services, lack of upcoming announcements or financial instability of the company. We also list disturbed relationships with analysts or the fact that no relationships exist yet with identified leading analysts. It should be noted in this context that this document is not intended for broad company internal communication. Thus, one should not try to hide existing weaknesses because it is believed that this impacts the morale of the employees. It is important to be honest and to name existing issues. Otherwise they can never be fixed.

In the "Opportunity" section we want to look forward. For example we may know of an upcoming announcement that should strengthen the company's position. This is obviously an opportunity we want to address in our communication with the industry analysts and we should be able to exploit it to influence their attitudes towards our company and/or our products. In this section we must not only look into company driven activities, but we may also be aware of opportunities that arise from the industry. Maybe one of our competitors is distracted because of a significant acquisition. Maybe a major event or a trade show is coming up that will allow us to position the company well. Or, maybe a changing political or legal situation works in our favor.

Finally, in the "Threats" section we list all known facts that could cause issues in the near future. We may anticipate a major move from one of our competitors, maybe our products are late to the market or they have quality issues or a political or legal change may work to our disadvantage. We may also be aware of changes in the industry that our company is not prepared for yet. But there are also threats directly related to industry analyst relations. Maybe an analyst firm that is favorable towards our company is acquired by another firm and we are not sure yet if this will impact the relationship with them. Other threats may be the lack of spokespeople in the company dedicating time to meeting with analysts.

Please consider the above as food for thought only. The above examples should only indicate some of the facts that may influence the industry analyst program significantly. There are many other facts that may appear on your SWOT analysis depending on the respective situation of your company and the state of the industry your company operates in. When doing the SWOT exercise you need to pay attention not to narrow your view too much. Don't just pay attention to items driven by your company. Also pay attention to developments in the market, the industry in general and the analyst community. In fact, when listing strengths and weaknesses, one should focus on internal aspects. Opportunities and threats, however, are external.

Once the SWOT analysis is properly done all the facts are on the table. You now have the basis for drawing some initial conclusions. The SWOT analysis should have provided some indications on how to use the resources you have available in the industry analyst relations program. You will not be able to make final decisions yet about the priorities in the coming time, though, because you did not define the program's objectives yet. These will only be discussed in the following sub-chapter, since they are only derived from the situation analysis and the business objectives. Ultimately, the situation analysis and the objectives will drive the program implementation that will be discussed a bit later in this chapter.

### Objectives

This innocent looking sub-chapter will actually describe the core of the success or failure of your industry analyst relations program. Wrong objectives may lead to excellent results per the defined scorecard or metrics – and still the program was a failure since it did not contribute to the success of the business.

It is mandatory that the objectives are aligned with the overall business objectives and the marketing/communication objectives of the company (which, in return, are also derived from the business plan). Thus, the objective of the industry analyst relations program should directly support the business objectives. There is no space for "academic" objectives like for example maintain excellent relationships with leading analysts. Such an objective can only be the prerequisite for a more strategic objective. It should be understood that analysts may have an excellent personal relationship with an industry analyst relations manager or a senior executive – and still report negatively on the company.

The only exception may be during the start-up phase of the industry analyst relations program. During that time we may define objectives like identify leading analysts, create a good relationship with analysts or establish the program's infrastructure.

The most important point, however, is that objectives are precisely defined. You should not be able to interpret them in different ways. You should for example ask the question: What is a leading analyst? Is that an analyst who is quoted most often in the press or is that an analyst who has the best network or is that an analyst who consults with most customers – or is that an analyst who influences purchases with the highest values?

As already said above, communication objectives need to support business objectives. we would recommend to directly link the communication objectives to the respective business objective.

**Example:**

Business objective: Increase the business by 25 percent in developing markets.
Analyst relations program objectives:
Identify three analysts who focus on developing markets.
Identify the three most influential analysts based within the targeted markets.
Develop messaging specifically for developing markets.
Brief the analysts with local spokespeople from the targeted region.
Trigger positive coverage by every analyst, e.g. in research notes, in newsletters to clients or in interviews with the press within 3 months.

You may or may not agree with the objectives defined in this example. This is not important. It is more important to see the clear link to the business objective. The plan is not to work generically with analysts, but to target specifically those analysts that are influential in the target market.

The first objective ("identify three analysts who focus on developing markets") looks a bit out of context since there seems to be no follow-on activity defined. we have added it to the example since this could illustrate the cooperation with the planning team. The analyst relations team probably got the charter to identify those analysts to pass the leads over to the planning team to purchase consultancy from them.

It is important that all stakeholders in the analyst relations plan have an opportunity to review it before it is signed off. In real life a plan typically goes through several approval cycles. This approach is not only recommended to ensure consistency with other activities, but it also ensures that all stakeholders have a common understanding and a common expectation towards the program. In a typical "management by objectives" approach (MBO) stakeholders, management and analyst relations professionals jointly agree on the objectives. we would consider this approach to be crucial for the success of the program. The fifth objective ("trigger positive coverage") must be realistic and agreed to by all parties. It may be a realistic or an unrealistic goal depending on the state of the company. It may be unrealistic if the company is going through a severe crisis, for example. In that case, this objective should be revisited. This objective can also be discussed in the light of ethical questions (see appendix A).

In the above example the specific messaging to be used with the analysts was still to be defined. We may have to push out the messaging definition in special circumstances. It is much more appropriate, though, to define the messaging framework right away and include it into the plan. You would then only fine tune the messaging for a specific briefing depending on recent changes or specific needs. Still, you would always operate within the messaging framework that was defined in the very beginning and that is agreed also with the other departments in your organization.

You may also want to list all analysts covered by the program in this part of the plan. Alternatively, you document that list in an appendix to the plan.

### Implementation description

In this part of the plan we go into tactics. We want to define processes, tools and the program roll-out.

We certainly want to agree on communication processes within the company. To avoid delays and unnecessary email floods we want to agree on roles and responsibilities of all involved stakeholders. Responsibilities, accountabilities, approval rights etc are defined and agreed upon. Also, it needs to be clarified who needs to be consulted to come to agreements and who needs to be informed.

For example, we want to ensure that all communication to analysts is aligned and well documented. Presentations from different company departments may need to be cross-checked before delivered to the analysts. Materials delivered in earlier briefings or in briefings from different geographies should be stored to be consulted for consistency. And finally, we want to have a defined process to align materials shared with industry analysts with information shared with other target audiences.

All the tools listed in chapter 5 should also be documented in this chapter.

Ways of communication to the analysts is also documented in this part of the plan. Newsletters and briefings are listed. Also, spokespeople with their respective focus areas are agreed upon and listed in the plan.

In addition to these logistical details we also want to highlight planned campaigns and projects in the implementation description section. We will base our plans on the overall communication plan and the SWOT analysis we did in the situation analysis section.

Since this section is the core of our plan, we want to discuss a few examples. Hopefully they guide the reader in his or her own planning.

**Example 1:**
We know that our company will release a number of new powerful products in the spring timeframe. They will be announced at different dates across a time period of up to two months. – It is appropriate to brief analysts on the entire range of products in a single briefing, rather than trying to meet them several times across such a short timeframe. Delivering the entire story in one go will not only save the spokespeople's and the analysts' time, but will also make the announcement more powerful than delivering the news in pieces.

**Example 2:**
We observe an analyst to be doubtful about our company's future. The analyst has expressed several times that he is not convinced that the technology delivered by our company has a sustainable growth path, i.e. it would not be a safe investment for customers who need to plan for growth. – You plan a special visit for this analyst to your company's research and development facilities, where he can see first hand that your company is aggressively investing in future growth.

**Example 3:**
You need to create awareness for your company with an identified industry analyst firm. – In this case you have several options. A straightforward approach may be to set up meetings with high level executives from your company. Another approach would be to get actively involved in that firm's conferences. Typically, analyst firms offer companies to sponsor parts of their events, participate with an exhibition or with a spokesperson delivering a speech. Depending on the respective situation, we personally would prioritize to explore the availability of a speaking opportunity.

**Example 4:**
Analysts tend to visit the key industry events addressing the topic they are measured against. Therefore, we may want to take advantage of the fact that our company will participate at such an industry event like e.g. a trade show. We may want to invite them to our booth before the formal opening of the show and give them an exclusive guided tour or provide a brief update on the company's latest developments.

**Example 5:**
We anticipate that one of our strongest competitors will announce a powerful new series of products well before our own since we had to delay the rollout of our products due to unexpected issues in manufacturing. – Quietly

watching our competitor eating our lunch may not be a good idea. We should plan for a communication of a special message to the analysts providing them with early information on our own future offering. Ideally we preempt our competitor, so the analyst is already aware of our plans when our competitor talks to them. However, we strongly discourage to attempt spreading "fud" (fear/uncertainly/doubt) against the competition. This approach is not sustainable and will move you into a defensive position immediately. Constructive content is certainly more useful. It could be first results from beta testers or early access customers of your coming products.

We hope that these examples show that an analyst relations manager has a broad portfolio of tactical tools he can select from. The challenge is to agree on the right ones in this planning process.

### Metrics

In the following chapter we will go into the details of how to measure an industry analyst relations program. You will have to define a subset of measures that is agreed upon and entered into the industry analyst relations program.

It is important that the criteria are in line with the objectives defined above.

When introducing the metrics you need to ask yourself the question what you actually want to measure. You obviously want to measure the effectiveness of the program to ensure that you get a proper return on the investment. In addition you have the opportunity to measure the performance of the individual employees. It needs to be clearly understood that this would be based on different parameters. For example, the employees perform well, but the program still does not provide the expected results. This could be caused by issues that cannot be influenced by the individual employees, like for example a company crisis. On the other hand, a positive result could hide the fact that an employee could have been even more effective.

Individual performance measures must not be put into the plan. They belong into personal evaluation activities. In our program plan we want to focus on program effectiveness against the initial objectives. The criteria should be defined in a way that the results allow an objective picture of how the company is perceived by the analyst community.

Finally, measures like analyst satisfaction with program logistics are not very valuable. They do not allow a translation to analyst attitudes. You want to focus on measuring the impact you are making on your company's bottom line. You do not necessarily want to measure basics like e.g. the analysts' satisfaction with your information delivery.

# Chapter 7:

## Measuring An Industry Analyst Program

We want to start this chapter with a comparison between analyst relations and press relations.

We have learned in PR that the results of a PR program can be measured on different levels. We can measure basics on an "output level". This includes parameters like the number of published articles or the number of journalists attending a press conference. We can also measure on a more sophisticated level, the "outgrowth level", if the message a company wanted to promote was actually understood and communicated in the intended way. And finally we can measure the holy grail, the change of customer behavior as a result of the PR work. This final level is called the "outcome level" in Walter Lindenmann's model.

A similar approach can be taken when measuring an industry analyst relations program. we will discuss measurement schemes on three levels similar to what has been introduced for PR.



### Basics

Before we go any further with an analyst relations program we need to understand if we have identified the right analysts in our industry. In order to do so we need to understand the market our company is present in and we need to segment the customers who are potential targets for our company. We need to develop an understanding of the drivers in our customers' purchase decisions and we need to identify the importance of industry analysts per customer segment.

Once that is done we identify the analyst firms and the respective analysts themselves. The sources for that kind of information are obvious. Our customers will tell us whose opinion they respect. We will find analysts quoted in the press. And – in informal discussions – we will learn from analysts, who they consider to be their own competitors, i.e. they may tell us about potential new additions to our program's target audience.

Additional information is available by consulting analyst relations agencies or simply by visiting the website www.analystprofiles.com, a service provided by the company Tekrati (see also the appendix on useful references).

It is mandatory for an analyst program to identify at least what we called tier 1 analysts in chapter 5.

In order to secure a constant flow of information to the identified analysts it may then be useful to measure basic parameters like the number of contacts with the analysts. This, however, can only be a very basic measure since there is no linear dependency between number of contacts and analyst satisfaction. (And even if we were able to make that link, we would still have a long way to go to track their attitude and their attitude change over time as a result of the analyst relations program.) Too many contacts may even annoy the analyst. Thus, this measure should only be considered to be a basic indicator for the fact that analysts receive information on an ongoing basis through the analyst relations program.

You should consider to set specific goals for tier 1 analysts like meeting them face-to-face at least once a year or even once a quarter – depending on the amount of news that can be shared and depending on the need of the analysts.

One additional basic measure would be an extension to your existing PR measures. Your regular media analysis should include a report on analyst quotes picked up in the press. Ideally that report does not just provide a figure like "in May, 15 analyst quotes were found in the press". Ideally that report lists the names of the analysts and also their respective quotes. These quotes do not only tell us something about the analysts' opinions, they also tell us something about their visibility and it tells us something about existing networks between journalists and analysts. Over time you will find that a journalist has a tendency to go to their "favorite analyst" whenever he needs a second opinion on a topic he writes about. Turning the argument around this obviously means that if you have a special interest in being well covered in a certain publication you want to work closely with the analyst who tends to be consulted by that publication.

In this context we need to make some comments on an inappropriate extension to an existing PR measurement program.1 In PR, the so-called "share-of-voice" measure is a very common visualization of the results of a PR program. Share of voice compares the number of mentions of companies in the media. Even in PR it is already questionable when this measure is based simply on volume without considering the importance of a publication, i.e. its circulation and the audience it reaches out to. As soon as share of voice is based on impressions taking into account the publications' respective circulations it becomes a more valuable tool. Applying share of voice to the industry analyst relations world requires a similar sophistication. If the share of voice evaluation only counts analyst quotes in the media or mentions in the analysts' respective research collateral then the tool is basically useless. An analyst influencing a purchase volume of $1m would count as much as an analyst who influences $1bn. Later in this chapter we will see a first approach to take into account the importance of an analyst.

An additional issue of the share of voice measure is the fact that it only measures quantities. It does not measure the tonality expressed in the articles. If the tonality is negative, for example, you would aim at having a low share of voice turning the underlying assumption of a share of voice result upside down…

Probably a more sophisticated basic measure would be to count the number of queries coming in from industry analysts. Why are queries a measure for the success of an analyst program? The answer is that analysts would not bother to raise queries if they did not expect an answer. Thus, a query indicates trust in the industry analyst relations program – apart from the fact that it keeps the dialogue going. Again, it needs

[1] See also: "Under the Influence: Five Reasons to Worry About 'Share of Voice' Metrics" by Stephen England on ARmadgeddon (release 5.02 from 31 January 2006).

to be understood that there is no direct correlation between analyst satisfaction and the number of queries raised by the analyst. Receiving many queries does not directly indicate satisfaction with your program, neither does a low number of queries imply that the analyst has no trust in you. The parameter "number of queries raised" should always be seen in combination with additional information.

For example, you may have a process in place that measures your response time to the analyst. It is highly recommended, by the way, to measure that number just like most support centers measure the time to get back to a customer who has filed a question or a concern.

Analyst programs with a poor response time typically receive less queries than those with fast turnaround times. In this case, a high number of queries indeed indicates trust in the program. The analyst knows he will get a reply in an appropriate timeframe. But what is appropriate? Certainly we do not look into response times we are used to in PR. A journalist tends to work against very tight deadlines. Generally an analyst is more flexible – unless he requires it immediately to consult a customer appropriately. He may need same-day replies in some cases. In other cases, where intensive data mining is needed, an analyst easily accepts a response time of days or even weeks.

Until now we have only looked at numbers. We did not look into the nature of the queries yet. It may be needless to say that the matter of the queries has a strong influence on the interpretation of the number of queries. A high number of "normal" questions like request for specific product information or shipment data should indicate trust in the program (even though a too high number may indicate that your program should become more proactive and provide the requested data upfront). A high number of questions revealing a negative attitude like e.g. "Why didn't you tell customers that they can't use your product like this?" may indicate a crisis, though.

We guess the above can be summarized like this:

If analysts rate your program high (e.g. in an annual survey), then the number of incoming queries from analysts not only shows their interest in the company and its products, but it also indicates trust in getting a proper response within an appropriate timeframe. A decrease of incoming queries should be considered to be an early warning sign for potential problems. It may indicate a decreased interest in the company. On the other hand, it may also indicate that your program has improved its pro-activeness making additional queries redundant.

Basic measures as discussed above are particularly relevant during the initial phase of setting up a new industry analyst relations program. During these early stages our objectives are typically very basic as well. We want to establish the appropriate infrastructure for our program, we want to learn about our target audience and we want to prepare our organization for things to come.

We can basically separate company internal criteria from external measures. Examples for internal criteria are knowledge of the analyst landscape, have company spokespeople trained and prepared for briefings, response times to analyst queries.

Examples for external criteria are share of voice (taking into account tonality and influence of analysts) and quotes in the media.

### Attitude change

On an elevated level you certainly want to measure the influence you have on analysts' opinions.

Does the fact that you dedicated time and money to helping analysts getting information about your company and your products change their opinion on them?

Even though this question is an obvious one, it is a very delicate one at the same time. The reason for that lies in the ethical foundation of the industry analyst relations profession. The Code de Lisbonne (15 May 1991) states that no PR professional should agree to a contractual agreement with a client or an employer in which its success is measured against certain results. In particular, this code demands that a PR professional refrains from committing an editorial article in a defined magazine. In the same way, it does not approve to have a communications professional be measured against "brain washing" a journalist. In other words, PR professionals must not commit to an outcome that is beyond their control. Applying the same principle to analyst relations (see also Appendix A) means that an analyst relations professional must not be measured against changing analysts' opinions nor against any of their actions like writing a positive research note or a white paper after a briefing. This approach would be similar to a common mistake in PR demanding to "place an article"...

In other words: An analyst's opinion is not directly controlled by an analyst relations program. Analysts are always independent per definition. Their attitude towards companies, products and services is not dependent on their relationships with the respective company. However, a good industry analyst relations program can ensure that no opinion has been formed by an analyst based on incorrect or missing information.

The conclusion from the above should not be, though, not to measure analysts' opinions and attitudes. You still want to do that. However, you need to set the appropriate goals and you need to interpret the results appropriately. You do not want to be measured against changing the attitude of a specific analyst. You may still want to track the attitudes of individual analysts. But it would not be appropriate to make an analyst relations program solely responsible for them.

Now that we have understood how to interpret the results of an attitude survey, we return to the question how to actually gain that information. The main challenge you will face is to translate a qualitative measure into quantitative data that can be compared with the investment into an analyst relations program.

There are several ways of learning about industry analysts' opinions. One is to evaluate the analysts' output like research notes. Another one is to initiate a survey. In this case a questionnaire would be sent out to the analysts on a regular basis. A comparison of the answers in different surveys would then indicate changes over time. It is important to take into account that this measure requires time. Such a questionnaire could not be sent on a weekly nor monthly basis. we recommend to do such a survey only on an annual basis.

The questionnaire should have a very limited number of questions. Otherwise analysts would not bother spending the time to fill it in. Also, in order to allow a comparison over time the questions should be identical and they should not refer to day-to-day business.1

We recommend to develop a set of questions along the lines of the following criteria:

- Ask to rate the quality of the analyst program on a given scale.
- Ask to rate the analyst program vs. the competition in the industry.
- Ask if in their opinion of the company's position has changed over time (and why).

And, most importantly, allow for comments in the survey.

By the way, the number of responses to the survey itself is an indicator for the expectation level of the analysts. A low number may signal low interest in your company (either because it is not in their research scope – i.e. the analyst program targets the wrong analysts – or because they have no expectation that taking the time responding to the survey will result in any positive changes). A high response rate shows a genuine interest and it signals that the analysts considered it worthwhile to spend the time to provide feedback.

Before we continue the attempt to develop a parameter that indicates the performance of an analyst relations program, we want to introduce a visual way of summarizing our findings. we should be able to make a statement on two parameters for all analysts or analyst firms that we target with an industry analyst relations program. Firstly, we want to make a statement on their attitude towards the company, i.e. we want to rate their opinion on the company and/or the products and services it brings to market. Secondly, we want to know how much they actually know about the company and its products and services. These two parameters allow us to define a two-dimensional diagram, where we can display all analysts or analyst firms (see figure 7.1).

Ideally, all analysts are on a line from the lower left to the upper right. If so, we should be able to conclude that the more an analyst knows about the company the more positive he reports on it. In other words, we need to "educate" those analysts in the lower left hand corner to move them to the upper right hand quadrant – which is obviously the quadrant we prefer all targeted analysts to be in.

In return, we have a significant issue with analysts being in the lower right hand quadrant. They know the company very well, but apparently have come to the conclu-

---

[1] You certainly do not want to ask them for their opinion on that recent product announcement of your company, for example. Some analysts would not appreciate such a direct question anyway, since they would expect you to formally consult with them to get access to their opinion. Questions like that should only be asked in a one-on-one situation where information is shared in both directions.

sion that they do not appreciate what they have seen. They have developed a negative attitude and it will be our task to identify the cause of that attitude before we can actually address it. It may be based on true issues the company is facing, it may be based on false communication, it may be based on misunderstandings, it may be based on successful PR from the competitors – just to name a few reasons.

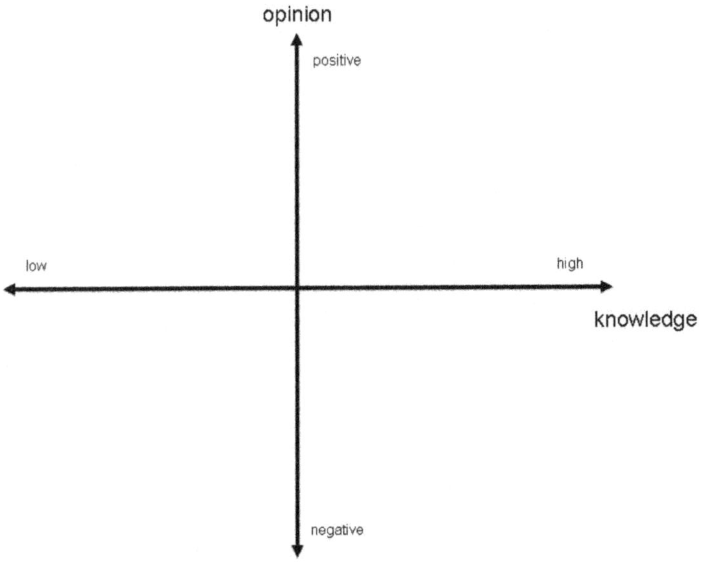


**Figure 7.1:** Expertise-attitude-diagram

The figure 7.1 gives us a qualitative way of describing the state of our relations with industry analysts. HFN Analyst Relations (see also appendix C) proposes a more sophisticated diagram splitting the x-axis (or "knowledge-axis") into four phases. In their approach the x-axis actually becomes a relationship-axis describing the relationship between analyst and vendor. The four phases on that axis range from basic awareness on the left hand side to close contacts on the right. In other words, an analyst's knowledge about a vendor's offering has been replaced by a measure for the relationship between analyst and vendor. This visualization of the work done by an industry analyst relations manager is actually very similar to the perception grid proposed to measure the results of PR (see figure 7.2). This grid should ideally show that an increased proactive work of the PR (or industry analyst relations) manager should impact a journalist's (or analyst's) attitude towards his or her company and/or products and services.

In diagram 7.2 we want to see the analysts we work with ideally on the right hand side. An analyst in the upper right hand corner is positive, but we need to invest a lot of work in getting or keeping them there. An analyst in the lower right hand corner apparently does not require a lot of "maintenance". They may be at risk, however, to change attitude, since we only put a minimum investment into the relationship with them.

| PROACTIVE OUTREACH | | | | |
|---|---|---|---|---|
| | **Consistent & Frequent** | | | |
| | **Somewhat Regular** | | | |
| | **Sporadic** | | | |
| | | **Negative** | **Receptive** | **Publicly Positive** |
| | | ATTITUDE TOWARD - OR PERCEPTION OF - YOUR COMPANY | | |

**Figure 7.2:** Perception grid

We now want to return to the survey we discussed above to drive the development of a quantitative measure.

When evaluating the responses of a survey it is important to ensure that the feedback from tier 1 analysts is weighed higher than that of lower level analysts. Per definition tier 1 analysts have the strongest impact on customers' buying behavior. Their feedback should outweigh that of lower level analysts. The degree of sophistication of a mathematical model depends on the level of existing information and the available resources in the analyst relations program – or the dedicated analysis team.

A simple approach would be to estimate a multiplier for a tier 1 analyst over a lower tier analyst. Say, this factor is 4. In this case, one happy – or positive – tier 1 analyst balances out 4 unsatisfied lower tier analysts, or: One tier 1 analyst has as much impact on your measurement parameter as four lower level analysts.

Let us assume we measure the analysts' opinion of your company on a scale from 0 to 1. 0 would indicate that the analyst's opinion is so negative that none of their clients would purchase your products. 1 would indicate that the opinion is so positive that he will convince all their clients to shortlist your products. Any value between 0 and 1 would then indicate the fraction of the business you could get from the overall amount the analyst influences.

The weighing factor we introduced above would then indicate the size of the influenced business. It is obvious that the introduction of a plain factor (like 4 in the above example) may only be a very rough estimate. If more detailed information is available then a very complex formula can be generated that contains the exact business amounts per analyst or per analyst firm.

The simplified formula to calculate the impact of an analyst program would be

$$I = \text{factor} \cdot \sum \text{opinion}(i) + \sum \text{opinion}(j)$$

where

opinion is an attitude measure (scaling between 0 and 1)1,
factor is an estimate for increased impact of a top tier analyst,
i indicates the top tier analysts,
j indicates the lower tier analysts.

The impact "I" in this formula really represents a satisfaction level of the analysts with your company. The value does not translate directly into a business volume that is impacted. This is so because we only estimated the relative impact of the analysts, but we did not include the absolute volumes of the impacted business per analyst or analyst firm.

The more sophisticated version of this formula would be

$$I = \sum \text{opinion}(i) \cdot \text{volume}(i) / \sum \text{volume}(i)$$

where

opinion is an attitude measure scaling between 0 and 1,
volume is the impacted business volume per analyst or analyst firm,
i indicates all analysts (i ranging from 1 to n),
n is the number of all analysts included in the program.

We notice that "I" this time is not only a measure for the averaged attitude, i.e. a relative measure, but "I" represents directly the fraction of the business that is positively influenced by the analyst relations program.

A little word of caution here, though: It would be incorrect to claim that the analyst relations program is responsible for generating a lead to get access to this business. It would be appropriate, though, to claim responsibility for an improvement of "I" be-

[1] Since we only calculate a relative measure here, it is not required to gauge the attitude measure to a scale from 0 to 1. But if you change the scale, you need to change the interpretation of us as well.

tween two measurements. In other words: The analyst relations program has created low(er) hanging fruit for the sales organization to benefit from.

**Example:**
Within one year the factor we improved from 0.5 to 0.6. This would be equivalent to getting access to an additional 10% of the business influenced by the analysts. If we assume the market size was $1bn, then the analyst program would be accountable for getting access to another $100m. These absolute numbers show the power of a strong industry analyst program.

It is very important to state in this context that the analyst program enables access to new business. It does not directly generate that additional business. To achieve that, we will still need a powerful sales force. The reason for that is that an analyst can obviously have very positive attitudes towards multiple companies, i.e. several could claim simultaneously that they have an "I" of 1. But the higher the value "I" is the easier it becomes for the sales force to turn a business lead into revenue. Here ultimately the loop from the introductory remarks in the book closes, we recognize and prove that the analyst relations program is a powerful sales support tool.

To calculate the proper ROI (return-on-investment) value the following considerations need to be taken into account. We assume that we invest a certain amount of money on the program. The return value consists of several line items including:

- Value of information collected from analysts during communication arranged by the analyst relations program.
- Equivalent investment in sales to have the same impact in lead generation.
- Profits from closed deals.

We would argue that in many cases a breakeven is achieved without even including the profits into the ROI equation.

**Exceptions**

The previous paragraphs show that an industry analyst program should be measured against the impact it makes with the company's customers. This obviously means that analyst firms that focus on vendors – rather than on users – should not be a focus of an industry analyst relations program at all.

While this is fundamentally correct, there are exceptions that may apply in certain special circumstances. we want to discuss one example here that illustrates such an exception.

We assume we work for a company in an emerging market in Central or Eastern Europe. The company is the leading reseller in its country. Unfortunately, there is no independent data that confirms the company's leading position – except the market share data of a local industry analyst firm. While market share data in a mature market is an exercise that is mainly looking backwards, it can have a very direct impact on a company's future under certain circumstances. Market share data may indicate trends in the industry or they may be the basis for measuring executives. In this specific case they may be the basis for additional business.

We assume that a foreign vendor is ready to enter our emerging market. They are looking for a distribution partner in our country. Our own company is very interested in working with that vendor, but needs to prove its strength to be selected as their partner. It becomes clear immediately that our company has a strong interest in the local analyst firm properly reporting its leadership position. And thus, an analyst relations manager in the company may be given the charter to focus on working closely with this analyst firm – despite the fact that this analyst firm does not address end users.

### Summary

We have seen that a direct translation of established PR metrics to the function of industry analyst relations may not be appropriate and needs to be handled with care. The reason for that is mostly the different nature of journalists and analysts. Their reach and their impact on customers are different. You may want to compare it with the difference between a shotgun and a precision gun. Journalists typically reach out to a broad audience that may only be vaguely defined. Analysts are much more targeted. To a large degree we understand who they consult with and we know that their impact on their clients is not comparable with the impact that an editorial story makes on them.

As a result, we can take advantage of statistical approaches in measuring PR. But measuring industry analyst relations needs to be much more qualitative than quantitative. We should consider to put figures behind the amount of purchases influenced by analysts as seen above, but we also need to pay attention to soft metrics like measuring the relationships with the analysts1. A very important factor is for example the trust level the analyst puts into your company.

Still, we can continue to measure an analyst relations program on the same three levels that have been defined by Walter Lindenmann for PR. We can measure on an output, an outgrowth and an outcome level. In the case of industry analysts, the outgrowth and the outcome levels are significantly closer

1 A final word of caution here, though! We are advocates for measuring relationships in PR. But we need to be aware of the fact that measuring relationships in industry analyst relations can only be a secondary measure. Analyst may personally like you, but still write negative comments about your company. Still, it may be fair to say that a positive relationship with an analyst is a solid foundation for further steps, while a bad relationship makes it so much more difficult to have them recommend your company and its products and services to his clients.

together than in the case of PR, though. Once an analyst understood a company's message he will be able to communicate it to their clients in the appropriate way and their clients, in return, will indeed very seriously consider the inputs in their purchasing decisions.

We want to summarize this chapter in a few recommendations you may want to consider for your own industry analyst relations program:

- Before you measure you have to agree on goals.
- Evaluation should not become a complex science.
- Be aware of the fact that you can measure on different levels.
- Subjective measures must be avoided.
- Qualitative measures should dominate in analyst relations (rather than quantitative measures).
- A straightforward adoption of methods from other communication functions (like PR) cannot always be recommended.
- Results should be incorporated into future planning.
- Measures at different times must be comparable.

## Appendix A:

## Industry Analyst Relations – The Cause Of Conflicts Of Interest?

In January 2006 Forbes published an article (The String Pullers, by Chris Kraeuter) that discusses the power of industry analyst firms. The article discusses the case of a software company that puts a significant amount of money into fees to research firms like Gartner, Forrester and others. In addition, the company invests quite significantly in industry analyst relations. The question is raised if all that investment is actually justified.

The underlying question, though, goes beyond that. The power of industry analysts influencing customers' spending is well understood. It is basically asking if industry analyst firms can be compromised, since their business model makes them take money from their clients as well as from vendors. Would they still be objective, or can vendors influence their opinions making themselves significant clients of industry analyst firms?

Other sources even go beyond the above and list additional facts that could be the cause for analysts having a conflict of interest.

One potential issue is the fact that industry analysts do paid consulting work for vendors. Can analysts still be neutral when they have potentially even been involved in defining a vendor's strategy, the positioning of its products or the messaging to the public? Would analysts treat clients the same way as other vendors – or would they be prejudiced? Why should they comment negatively on a vendor's message if they themselves have been part of the process to define it?

Along with the above goes the fact that industry analysts most likely have access to confidential information of their clients. It must be a difficult task to consider that information in their role as consultant for a vendor, but to ignore it when researching the very same vendor. You might argue that to some degree this requires a schizophrenic approach.

The practice of many analyst firms to publish white papers in cooperation with vendors may also be a questionable exercise. Often enough these white papers are signed only by the analyst firm, even though the content was agreed and approved by the vendor. Such documents are typically fully paid for by the vendor, but they leave the impression of being the result of independent research. Again, the question comes up if an analyst firm can still call itself to be independent when they contribute to a vendor's marketing collateral.

One final issue we want to bring up in this context is the fact that many industry analyst firms allow their employees to hold stock of vendors they consult and their competitors. Does this result in a biased approach of the individual analysts towards their clients?

We are convinced that the above questions need to be taken very seriously. And we are convinced that it is especially the analyst firms that are taking them extremely seriously. It is probably needless to say that the biggest asset of an analyst firm is not necessarily the information it has access to, but its integrity. An analyst firm simply cannot afford to spoil its reputation, since this would immediately impact their business significantly.

At a Forrester event in London in December 2005 Martha Bennett phrased it very clearly: There is no pay for play. She highlighted that "analysts do not want to hear comments like 'we would like to brief you, but we're also evaluating analyst firms that we might want to work with". In return "vendors do not want to hear 'you have got an interesting product here, but unfortunately you're not a client".

A little comment in Louis Columbus' book "Getting Results From Your Analyst Relations Strategies" makes us wonder, however, if the above is followed by all analysts. In the context of vendor-to-analyst briefings, Columbus states that "the goal is to have the analysts speak more than you do; get them to open up and give you both their opinions." we fully agree with this approach. A briefing should in fact be a dialogue if ever possible. But then Columbus continues that "that is what you are paying for." This seems to imply that a vendor has to pay for briefing an analyst. If that is indeed what is meant we would not be in agreement. Just like a consultant should not pay for having the privilege to consult with a customer, an analyst should offer appropriate free time for receiving information. Ultimately this information is the basis for being successful in their profession as an analyst. Or, in other words: Accepting information only from paying vendors would no longer allow an analyst to position themself as independent. His clients would no longer be able to expect independent consulting.

Some analyst firms have taken active measures and try to control potential risk by consciously diversifying their client base, so that no single vendor has a significant impact on the company's bottom line. Others limit the time of individual analysts being paid by individual companies.

Many companies insist that they separated their sales department sufficiently from their analysts to avoid analysts from being impacted by the financial aspect in the relationship with a vendor. we are not entirely convinced if we agree with the effectiveness of this measure since that very same analyst is typically measured and compensated against selling their time. But this approach is certainly supporting the comments we made in chapter 2 on the communication flow between a vendor and an analyst firm (see subchapter on industry analyst relations and business planning).

The industry analyst relations department is not supposed to work with the sales department of an analyst firm. As soon as that communication line dominates the relationship between the two companies, a flood gate would be opened allowing many of the concerns discussed above to become reality.

So, how can an industry analyst relations program contribute to maintaining the integrity of industry analysts?

We have already seen that an analyst program should operate in parallel to the company's planning or business intelligence team. "In parallel" implies that both programs should be independent from each other, but they should cooperate. For example, if an analyst firm needs to be sourced for consulting, the analyst relations team can help identifying candidates. All negotiations with the analyst, however, should be done by the planning team. Vice versa, the planning team can share purchased research with the analyst relations team (if the terms of the subscription service allows to do so). This would allow an analyst relations manager to learn about the analysts' fields of interest, their attitudes, etc. Consulting work done by an analyst for a vendor should always be managed by the business intelligence team. The analyst relations manager should be aware of it but not be involved, nor must he refer to that in any outbound communication.

Forrester's Chief Strategy and Marketing Officer Brian Kardon commented in the Forbes article we referred to above that the vendor-analyst relationship should be managed similar to the vendor-press relationship. You want to manage the relationship with the press also in two parallel communication lines, one being PR and the other one being advertising. You certainly want to avoid making the results of your PR work dependent on your advertising budget and, vice versa, publishing houses want to avoid an impact on revenue from advertising due to their published editorial content.

The strongest contribution the industry analyst relations program can make to avoid compromising industry analysts – and their own company – is to agree on a clear understanding of the own role: Industry analyst relations is not about selling. It is not about passing an opinion on to an analyst. It is about passing facts to analysts so they can draw their own conclusions and form their own opinions.

In January 2007, the German Analyst Relations workgroup (DARA) agreed to articulate an ethics code that summarizes what is expected of an industry analyst relations professional. The code addresses the behavior of both, an in-house industry analyst relations manager as well as that of an employee of a consultancy. The code is based on the Lisbon code of ethics (11 May 1991) for PR professionals. It contains 21 articles covering general aspects as well as a code of conduct towards employers or clients, towards industry analysts and towards colleagues and competitors.

Louis Columbus discusses a whole different aspect of ethics related to an analyst transitioning from his role as an analyst to a new job offered to him by a vendor[1]. This is indeed another aspect that justifies some investigation. However, in the context of the discussions we have here, we would to reduce this topic to only a few remarks. An analyst obviously has a lot of information that may be very useful to a vendor – but so do employees from competitors. we would expect analysts to respect proprietary information just like other employees do when they move on from one employer to another one. If a vendor intends to buy a lead generator, then a move is beneficial for neither party. The analyst will regret the move very soon, and the vendor will not get what he tried to get, as long as all rules are followed.



[1] Getting Results From Your Analyst Relations Strategies, Louis Columbus, LWC Research – e-book available as PDF document (November 2004), ISBN: 0-595-33462-8

# Appendix B:

## Analyst Firms

In this appendix we provide an overview of most major analyst firms – with a special focus on the European market. The information provided here contains a list of the firms, a basic summary of the company's services and a website URL (as of April 2007) that allows the reader to hunt for more detailed information. we hope that this summary provides a good starting point for communication professionals who are challenged to start an industry analyst relations program. A list like the following can never be complete, so we apologize upfront to any significant industry analyst firm we have overlooked when compiling the below list.

**Aberdeen Group Website:**
**www.aberdeen.com**
Aberdeen was founded it 1988. The headquarter is in Boston, Massachusetts. Their focus is on research and market trend analysis. Aberdeen addresses dynamics underlying specific technology-enabled business strategies and technology solutions.

**ABI Research Website:**
**www.abiresearch.com**
ABI's global headquarter is based in New York. The company was founded in 1990. Initially they addressed the wireless semiconductor components market. Since, they have expanded their coverage.

**Access Markets International (AMI) Partners Website:**
**www.ami-partners.com**
AMI is based in New York. They specialize in the global analysis of IT, internet and telecom trends in the global SMB[1] marketplace. (Do not mix them up with the Canadian company AMI Partners Investment Counsel!)

**Aite Group Website:**
**www.aitegroup.com**
Aite Group LLC is based in Boston, Massachusetts. They address the financial services industry providing advice on IT, business and regulatory issues.

**American Technology Research Website:**
**www.amtechresearch.com**
American Technology Research's main location is in San Francisco. They are also present in Denver and in Greenwich, Connecticut. They have multiple research focus areas including semiconductors, video gaming software and medical devices.

[1] SMB – Small and Medium Businesses

**AMR Research Website:**
**www.amrresearch.com**

AMR Research was founded in 1986. They focus on supply chain, enterprise applications and infrastructure. The firm is based in Boston, Massachusetts.

**Analysys Research Website:**
**www.analysis.com**

Analysys is a European firm with over 130 staff. The headquarter is in Cambridge, UK. Other office include Madrid, Milan and Paris. They provide strategy and management consultancy, information services and start-up support in the telecom, IT and media markets.

**ARC Advisory Group Website:**
**www.arcweb.com**

The ARC Advisory Group was founded in 1986 in the USA. The company addresses manufacturing and supply chain solutions.

**Argus Research Company Website:**
**www.argusresearch.com**

The U.S. based company is part of the Argus Research Group. They position themselves as an independent investment research firm. However, they are not just a financial analysis firm, since they also address industry analysis.

**Berlecon Research GmbH Website:**
**www.berlecon.de**

Berlecon is a German industry analyst firm founded in 1997. It specialized in analyzing new technologies for IT decision makers, vendors, government institutions and consultancies. The company's headquarters is in Berlin.

**Bloor Research Website:**
**www.bloor-research.com**

Bloor Research is based in Towcester, UK. The company was founded in 1989. Bloor provides a range of services for product vendors as well as end users based on a broad IT industry knowledge.

**Burton Group Website:**
**www.burtongroup.com**

The Burton Group is a U.S. based company providing decision support related to IT architecture and infrastructure topics to enterprises in multiple industries.

**Butler Group Website:**
**www.butlergroup.com**

This IT analyst company was founded in 1990 by Martin Butler. Their headquarter is in Hull in the UK. The Butler Group is a wholly owned subsidiary of Datamonitor (see below).

**Cambashi Website:**
**www.cambashi.com**

Cambashi is a European analyst firm based in Cambridge, UK. They operate within a global network of firms complementing each other. Cambashi has a focus on IT infrastructures for the industry including supply chain, engineering solutions and for example CAD.

**Cambridge Energy Research Associates (CERA) Website:**
**www.cera.com**

CERA Ltd. Is an advisor to energy companies, governments, financial institutions and technology providers. Their headquarter is in Cambridge, Massachusetts with additional offices around the globe. CERA has over 200 staff.

**Canalys Website:**
**www.canalys.com**

Canalys was founded in 1998 and is privately owned. Its headquarter is in the UK (Reading, Berkshire). Canalys' work is spanning IT, consumer electronics and telecommunications.

**Celent Website:**
**www.celent.com**

Celent LLC was founded in 1999. The U.S. based company is focused the application of information technology in the financial services industry. Celent provides research and consulting on the topic.

**CMS Watch Website:**
**www.cmswatch.com**

CMS Watch was founded in 2001 to provide independent advice on content management and search technologies. The company is based in Olney, Maryland.

**Compete Website:**
**www.compete.com**

The Boston, Massachusetts, based company positions itself as a predictive analytics company. Compete, Inc. They focus on analyzing and predicting consumer purchasing behavior.

**ContactBabel Website:**
**www.contactbabel.com**

ContactBabel is a UK based firm dedicated to the CRM industry. They provide research, analysis and business recommendations to CRM and contact centre solution providers.

**Context Website:**
**www.contextworld.com**

The London (UK) based company is around since 1983, when it was founded by Jeremy and Howard Davies. Context analyses business and consumer technology markets serving vendors, users and analyst communities.

**Current Analysis Website:**
**www.currentanalysis.com**

Current Analysis, Inc. is based in Sterling, Virginia. The company provides analysis, intelligence and advice to IT equipment vendors, service providers and IT buyers. Offices are in Washington, San Diego and Paris.

**Datamonitor Website:**
**www.datamonitor.com**

Datamonitor is headquartered in London, UK. The business information company addresses the automotive, energy, financial services, healthcare and technology industries as well as consumer markets.

**DisplaySearch Website:**
**www.displaysearch.com**

DisplaySearch is a member of the NPD Group (the U.S. based partner of GfK – see below). They compile shipment data and related information for display products like LCD monitors. Their clients are mainly vendors.

**Disruptive Analysis Website:**
**www.disruptive-analysis.com**

The London, UK, based business advisory firm was founded in 2002. Disruptive Analysis provides analysis and consulting support to users, vendors and others in the area of communications and information technology. The company has a focus on mobile and wireless solutions.

**Edison Group Website:**
www.theedison.com

The Edison Group is based in New York. The company provides competitive product and market intelligence addressing mainly IT product vendors.

**Eduventures Website:**
**www.eduventures.com**

The Boston, Massachusetts, based company positions itself as an information services company for the education market providing research and analysis to make purchase decisions and to improve operational performance.

**Enterprise Management Associates Website:**
**www.enterprisemanagement.com**

EMA's headquarter is in Boulder, Colorado. One of EMA's main focus areas is addressing the issues of management of technology, including hardware, software and services.

**Enterprise Strategy Group (ESG) Website:**
**www.enterprisestrategygroup.com**

The Milford, Massachusetts, based company was formerly known as the Enterprise Storage Group. They provide services to technology vendors, IT professionals, venture capitalists and institutional investors, mainly related to information management and storage.

**EuroLAN Research Website:**
**www.eurolanresearch.com**

This London, UK, based firm was founded in 1993. The company employs industry analysts and consultants who specialize in assisting technology companies transform their channel and alliance partnerships.

**Experton Group Website:**
**www.experton-group.com**

The Experton Group is a comparatively young company that was formed in 2005. They have offices in Germany, the Middle East and in the USA. The company provides consulting services, market surveys and other services such as conferences and seminars.

**Experture Website:**
**www.experture.com**

Experture is a group of independent analysts and consultants providing a wide range of services from contract negotiation support across traditional IT analysis and product comparisons to outsourcing support and other topics.

**Ferris Research Website:**
**www.ferris.com**

Ferris Research, Inc. is a San Francisco based research institute focused on messaging and collaborative technologies. Their clients are mainly technology vendors.

**Financial Insights Website:**
**www.financial-insights.com**

Financial Insights is a comparatively young company formed in 2002 by combining Meridien Research and IDC's (see for IDC below) Financial Services Advisory Business. The company provides information on technologies to the financial services companies.

**Forrester Research Website:**
**www.forrester.com**

Forrester is a global technology research company headquartered in Cambridge, Massachusetts. The company was formed in 1983. It provides research and advice about the impact of technology on business and consumers. Forrester had acquired the Giga Information Group. As of 2005 they consult with more than 2,000 client companies.

**Freeform Dynamics Website:**
**www.freeformdynamics.com**

Freeform Dynamics is an industry analyst and research company that focuses on the business impact of developments in the IT and communications markets across Europe and the US. The company was formed in 2005 and is based in the UK.

**Frost & Sullivan Website:**
**www.frost.com**

Frost & Sullivan was founded already in 1961. A European headquarter is based in London. They provide market intelligence with a focus to identify new opportunities for corporate growth. The company employs more than 1,000 analysts and consultants worldwide.

**Gartner Website:**
**www.gartner.com**

Gartner is the world's largest analyst firm. Gartner was founded in 1979 and acquired several smaller analyst companies over the years including Dataquest in 1995, Datapro Information Services in 1997 and META Group in 2005. As of early 2006, they have about 3700 employees.

**GfK Marketing Services Website:**
**www.gfk.de or www.gfk.com (English)**

GfK is a worldwide market research institute with its roots in Nürnberg, Germany. The company cooperates with the analyst firm NPD Group in the U.S. The company provides market data across a wide range of industries with a focus on consumer markets.

**Heavy Reading Website:**
**www.heavyreading.com**

Heavy Reading is a U.S. based company with its headquarters in New York. The market research organization offers quantitative analysis of telecom technology to carriers, providers and vendors.

**Hewson Group Website:**
**www.hewson.co.uk**

Hewson Group was founded in 1989. The company runs offices in the UK and in Germany. The company puts a strong focus on the CRM market in Europe.

**Hurwitz & Associates Website:**
**www.hurwitz.com**

The company is based in Waltham, Massachusetts. Hurwitz & Associates is a consulting and research firm providing guidance for investment decisions to IT executives.

**IDATE Website:**
**www.idate.fr (or: www.idate.org)**

IDATE employs analysts and consultants specializing in the telecommunication, internet and media sectors in Europe. The company was founded in 1977 and is based in Montpellier, France.

**IDC Website:**
**www.idc.com**

IDC is a global provider of market intelligence, advisory services and events for the IT, telecom and consumer technology markets. The firm employs about 850 analysts in 50 countries (2006). They cooperate with local firms like BMI-TechKnowledge Group in South Africa.

**Ideas International Website:**
**www.ideasinternational.com**

Ideas was founded in 1981. Their headquarter is in Hornsby, New South Wales, Australia. The company acquired D.H. Brown Associates in 2004. Ideas International researches a broad spectrum across computing platforms, systems software, operating systems and others.

**Industry Analysts, Inc. Website:**
**www.industryanalysts.com**

Industry Analysts, Inc. is a U.S. based marketing and management consulting firm. They specialize in research and training program development for the office automation industry. The company was founded in 1974.

**In-Stat Website:**
**www.instat.com**

In-Stat is based in Scottsdale, Arizona. The company provides research, assessments and market forecasts of semiconductors and advanced communications equipment and services.

**Illuminata Website:**
**www.illuminata.com**

Illuminata is based in Nashua, New Hampshire. The company is around since 1993. The focus of Illuminata is to provide insight on network-savvy information technology to enterprise decision makers.

**Infonetics Research Website:**
**www.infonetics.com**

Infonetics is a market research and consulting firm specializing in data networking and telecom. They offer a series of services including quarterly market share and forecasting data. Infonetics' headquarters is located in California.

**Informa Telecoms & Media Website:**
**www.informatm.com**

Informa has offices in London (UK) and Westborough, Massachusetts. The company positions itself as a provider of business intelligence to global telecoms and media markets.

**InfoTech Website:**
**www.pbimedia-infotech.com**

InfoTech is a subsidiary of Access Intelligence, LLC. The company specialized in market intelligence for the telecom and IT industries. In addition to intelligence programs the company offers sales tools, training and other services.

**InfoTrends Website:**
**www.infotrends.com**

The company was formerly called InfoTrends/ CAP Ventures. They focus their market research and strategic consulting on the digital imaging and document solutions industry.

**Intelligent Business Reserch Services (IBRS) Website:**
**www.ibrs.com.au**

IBRS is based in Hazelbrook, New South Wales (Australia). The company addresses Australian mid sized organizations providing an interactive decision support service.

**Intelligentis Ltd. Website:**
**www. Intelligentis.com**

This UK based consulting and research firm provides services such as consulting, research and marketing support to the telecom industry and related communities.

**Juniper Research Website:**
**www.juniperresearch.com**

Juniper Research is a UK based analyst firm specializing in the telecom and media sectors. The company puts a special focus on mobile and wireless solutions.

**JupiterKagan Website:**
**www.jupiterresearch.com**

JupiterResearch was sold to Kagan in early 2006. Jupiter provides research, analysis and advice to help companies profit from the impact of the internet and emerging consumer technologies on their business. It needs to be seen if the acquisition by Kagan will have an impact on the company's direction.

**Kennedy Information Website:**
**www.kennedyinfo.com**

Kennedy was founded in 1970 and is based in Peterborough, New Hampshire. The company, a subsidiary of BNA Inc., provides professional services including management consulting, executive recruiting and investor relations.

**Lünendonk Website:**
**www.luenendonk.de**

Lünendonk GmbH is a European research firm based near Munich in Germany. Lünendonk is specialized in market research. They also analyze selected industries and companies. Their broad service portfolio also includes consulting services related to the information technology.

**Lyra Research Website:**
**www.lyra.com**

Lyra, founded in 1991, provides analysis focused on the imaging industry (printers, copiers, digital photography, etc). The company advises clients across the globe.

**Macehiter Ward-Dutton Ltd. Website:**
**www.mwdadvisors.com**

Macehiter Ward-Dutton is a UK based IT advisory firm. The company is specialized in IT business alignment and provides research, analysis and consulting services.

**Manufacturing Insights Website:**
**www.manufacturing-insights.com**

Manufacturing Insights is a subsidiary of IDC (see above). The company, based in Framingham, Massachusetts, is focused on providing advice on business technology and applications for the manufacturing industry.

**MZA Website:**
**www.mzaconsultants.com**

MZA provides multi-client research and custom projects in the telecom and IT industries on a European and a global level. The company, based in the UK, is operational since the late 1980's.

**NelsonHall Website:**
**www.nelson-hall.com**

NelsonHall is a European research and consultancy firm based in Bracknell, UK. The company specialized in the analysis of business process outsourcing. NelsonHall was established in 1998.

**Ovum Website:**
**www.ovum.com**

Ovum, a Datamonitor (see above) company, is headquartered in Europe with European offices in London, Paris and Cologne. The analyst and consulting firm positions itself as an advisor on telecom, software and IT services. They consult with large corporations, IT and software vendors and service providers, telecom operators and others. In July 2006 Ovum announced the acquisition of the U.S. based company Summit Strategies. Ovum also acquired Orbis Consulting Ltd., a specialist advisory firm in outsourcing.

**Pharmaceutical Business Review Website:**
**www.pharmaceutical-business-review.com**

This organization is a typical service provider to a defined vertical industry, in this case the pharmaceutical industry. Similar services exist for other verticals including the automotive industry or financial services.

**PhoCusWright Website:**
**www.phocuswright.com**

PhoCusWright, founded in 1994, is a travel, tourism and hospitality research firm. They compile data to support competitive decision making.

**Pierre Audoin Consultants (PAC) Website**
**www.pac-online.com**

PAC is a European research and consulting firm headquartered in Paris, France. The company specialized in the software and the IT services industry. Their clients include IT service and software suppliers, consultancies, financial services institutions and telecom suppliers.

**Point North Group Website:**
**www.ktowngroup.com**

The Point North Group was formerly known as K-Town Group. The company, based in Larchmont, New York, provides research and consulting on digital media strategy. They consult for example with marketing and sale groups.

**Pyramid Research Website:**
**www.pyramidresearch.com**

Pyramid Research is headquartered in Cambridge, Massachusetts. Since 1986 the company provides market analysis and consulting services to the global communications industry.

**Quocirca Website:**
**www.quocirca.com**

This UK based research and analysis firm is focused on providing market insight and knowledge to technology vendors and service providers.

**The Radicati Group, Inc. Website:**
**www.radicati.com**

The Radicati group is headquartered in Palo Alto, California. The company, founded in 1993, focuses on market research for the computer and telecommunication industries.

**RedMonk Website:**
**www.redmonk.com**

RedMonk is an international research and consulting firm for the IT industry. The company is built on the open source concept being financed by various sponsors (see also Wikibon below).

**Robert Frances Group (RFG) Website:**
**www.rfgonline.com**

RFG is headquartered in Westport, Connecticut. The company positions itself as business advisors to IT executives. Their goal is to consult on IT purchases aligning IT efforts with corporate business strategies.

**Select Website:**
**www.select.com.mx (Spanish)**

Select is a Mexican company. They provide analysis of the IT and telecom markets as well as consulting services in areas such as sales and marketing.

**The Sageza Group, Inc. Website: www.sageza.com**

The Sageza Group is headquartered in California. The research and consulting company provides strategic retainer services, go-to-market services and market watch services.

**Semico Research Corporation Website: www.semico.com**

Semico was founded in 1994 and is based in Phoenix, Arizona. The company specialized in marketing and consulting research in the semiconductor industry. They also offer industry conferences.

**Springboard Research Website: www.springboardresearch.com**

Springboard, formerly known as Knowledge Platform Research, is based in Singapore. The company offers a set of IT market research services for IT firms in the hardware, software, networking and services sectors.

**Stanford Group Company (SGC) Website: www.stanfordgroup.com**

SGC is based in Houston, Texas. An affiliate office is based in Zurich, Switzerland. The company provides research for several sectors including biotechnology and semiconductors.

**Stratecast Partners Website: www.stratecast.com**

Stratecast Partners is a fully owned subsidiary of Frost & Sullivan (see above). The company is based in San Antonio, Texas, and focuses on the communications industry supporting their clients in decision making and planning processes.

**Strategy Analytics Website: www.strategyanalytics.net**

The company is based in Boston, Massachusetts and addresses selected sectors including automotive electronics and multimedia, digital consumer, wireless strategies and enabling technologies.

**Strategy Partners Website: www.strategy-partners.com**

This European IT market research and advice firm is based in the UK. The company specialized in sectors including document and content management, workflow and business process management, enterprise resource planning and others.

**Synergy Research Group (SRG) Website:**
**www.srgresearch.com**

The market research firm SRG focuses on delivering market statistics in the networking and telecommunications industries.

**TechConsult Website:**
**www.techconsult.de (English and German)**

TechConsult GmbH was founded in 1992. The company is based in Kassel, Germany. They provide market research and consulting with a strong focus on vertical markets.

**Technology Business Research Website:**
**www.tbri.com**

Technology Business Research, Inc. is based in Hampton, Hew Hampshire. The company provides insights within the computer, software, telecom, mobility and professional services industries addressing sales, marketing, business development, finance and other levels of their clients.

**TekPlus Website:**
**www.tekplus.com**

TekPlus is a consultancy and industry analyst firm focusing on vendors and end-users in the healthcare, finance, utilities, automation and communications industries.

**10th Street Website:**
**www.10thstreet.com**

10th Street Advisors has specialized in the telecom products and services marketplace. The company is based in Mt View, California, and Boulder, Colorado.

**The 451 Group Website:**
**www.the451.com or www.the451group.com**

The industry analyst firm is headquartered in New York. It addresses clients including vendors, investors, service providers and end user organizations.

**The Strategic Counsel Website:**
**www.thestrategiccounsel.com**

This Canadian company was established in 1995. Its headquarter is in Toronto. They provide quantitative and qualitative research in several areas including market segmentation and competitive analysis. They also consult on crisis management, do advertising tracking and provide additional services.

**TowerGroup Website:**
**www.towergroup.com**

This research and consulting firm is headquartered in Needham, Massachusetts. TowerGroup is focused exclusively on the global financial services industry. They provide information services and advice.

**TPI Website:**
**www.tpi.net**

TPI was founded in 1989. The company advises in sourcing initiatives and strategies. They operate on a global basis with their headquarter being in The Woodlands, Texas.

**Verdict Research Website:**
**www.verdict.co.uk**

Verdict Research is a Datamonitor (see above) company based in London. The firm is focused on providing research and analysis on retailing.

**Wikibon Website:**
**www.wikibon.org**

Similar to RedMonk, Wikibon offers research based on the open source philosophy. The company is focusing on research on technology and business systems.

**Yankee Group Website:**
**www.yankeegroup.com**

The Yankee Group's headquarter is in Boston, Massachusetts. The company is a research and advisory firm focused on communications and networking technologies.

# Appendix C:

# Useful References

In this section you will find several links and references to organizations and individuals that may help you in your quest to establish an industry analyst relations program yourself.

The first part will address links to existing industry analyst relations websites from leading corporations. These should provide a good basis for developing your own website infrastructure addressing industry analysts. In later parts you will find references of agencies that specialized in industry analyst relations and some other useful information.

### Industry Analyst Relations Websites

Several industry analyst websites are password protected and often enough information for industry analysts or links to further websites for analysts can be found in the pressroom or newsroom websites. The below list of web pages was compiled in summer 2006.

**Alcatel:** www.alcatel.com/industry_analysts

**BMC:** www.bmc.com/BMC/Common/CDA/hou_Page_Generic/0,3465,8028426_8128268,00.html?c=homepage_left_resources_column&n=%20analysts_link_from_home_page&t=1204 (the URL is very complicated, but the analyst relations website is linked directly from BMC's homepage)

**British Telecom:** www.btplc.com/Thegroup/Industryanalysts/index.htm

**CA:** www3.ca.com/analyst

**Cisco:** www.cisco.com/web/about/ac78/about_cisco_industry_analyst_relations_home.html

**HP:** www.hp.com/hpinfo/analystrelations

**IBM:** https://www-03.ibm.com/itanalyst/crsite.nsf/pages/homepage?opendocument

**Intel:** link under www.intel.com/pressroom/contacts

**Lucent:** www.lucent.com/industryanalyst

**Microsoft:** www.microsoft.com/mscorp/itanalyst

**Motorola:** www.motorola.com/industryanalysts

**Siemens:** www.siemens.com/page/1,3771,1245841-1-15_0_0-192,00.html (contact information only)

**Sprint:** www3.sprint.com/IAR/User/user_login (login page to password protected portal only)

**Sun Microsystems:** www.sun.com/secure/aboutsun/media/analyst/

**Sybase:** www.sybase.com/industry_analyst

**Symantec:** enterprisesecurity.symantec.com/analyst

**Industry Analyst Relations Bodies**

In April 2006 the "Institute of Industry Analyst Relations" (IIAR) was founded in London. The organization is expected to focus on developing the basis for a better cooperation between analyst relations professionals and industry analyst firms. Information about the group can be found at *finance.groups.yahoo.com/group/analystrelations/* and at *www.analystrelations.org*.

The "Deutsche Analyst Relations Arbeitskreis" (DARA) is a German group of analyst relations professionals that explores ways to improve industry analyst relations activities in Germany. The group was founded in 2006 as a result of an initiative of the German agency HFN (based in Frankfurt). Information about the group can be found on the HFN website at *www.hfn-ar.de*. Additional information is available at *de.groups.yahoo.com/group/AR-Arbeitskreis/*.

**Industry Analyst Relations Consultancies**

Most PR agencies offer to manage industry analyst relations in addition to managing press relations. If you consider to outsource your analyst relations program to your PR agency, then pay attention to the skills your agency can provide. There is a significant difference between analyst relations being done by "normal PR professionals" and a consultancy running a special practice focused on industry analyst relations.

We want to apologize upfront for not being able to list every single firm here that offers industry analyst relations consulting. we have just selected a few companies that we consider to be among the most sophisticated players in the industry.

Several agencies and consultancies focus exclusively on industry analyst relations. we want to reference a few of them here as a sample. Industry analyst relations is often also offered by individual independent professionals who have established good relations with leading industry analysts in selected industries.

The companies we want to reference here are KCG (*www.knowledgecap.com*), Lighthouse (*www.lighthousear.com*), the Analyst Strategy Group (ASG, *www.analyststrategy.com*), Tiger Lily, Sunesis (www.sunesis-global.com), Prasada (*www.prasada.net*), the company HFN Analyst Relations (*www.hfn-ar.de*), Insight Marketing, OnPR and Eastwest Public Relations.

We separate the firms by those who provide advisory and those offering outreach services to analysts.

**Advisories:**

KCG ("The Knowledge Capital Group") offers a full range of services from trainings for spokespeople all the way to measuring the effectiveness of an industry analyst program. They also offer a certified analyst relations training. The company is based in Austin, Texas, but offers their services on a global basis.

Lighthouse is headquartered in London, UK, with 11 additional offices in the USA, Asia and in Australia. The analyst relations team is lead by Duncan Chapple, a former Ovum consultant and analyst. Over the years Duncan has contributed a lot to promoting and understanding industry analyst relations. It is fair to say that Lighthouse truly operates on a global basis.

ASG is a U.S. based company with offices in California (San Diego), Washington (Seattle) and Colorado (Denver). They focus on supporting vendors with their industry analyst program making the program measurable.

**Firms offering outreach services:**

Tiger Lily (*www.tigerlily.uk.com*) is a UK based firm based in Maidenhead. The company focuses on analyst relations and influencer marketing.

Other UK based analyst relations consultancies are Sunesis and Prasada. Sunesis, a part of the Bell Pottinger Group, is based in Harmondsworth and led by David Rossiter, an experienced professional in analyst relations. Prasada is headed by Lore Ridings who has a significant experience in industry analyst relations.

The company HFN is based in Frankfurt. They have a dedicated team of individuals that focuses exclusively on industry analyst relations. The company offers a set of trainings as well as industry analyst relations consultancy in three steps, from planning across execution all the way to measurement of IAR programs.

An example of an agency that focuses on industry analyst relations with dedicated resources is Insight Marketing. The company is based in the UK and part of the Chime Group of companies. Their company's website URL is *www.insightmkt.com*.

Other firms in this range are OnPR (onpr.com), based in Portland, Oregon, and Eastwest Public Relations in Singapore (www.eastwestpr.com). Both firms offer a wide range of services with industry analyst relations being one of them.

Online information is available from various sources. The following are examples of blogs on industry analyst relations:

- Duncan Chapple (see above) edits the blog Analyst Equity, Lighthouse Analyst Relations' blog, is located at analystequity.com.
- armadgeddon.blogspot.com is an anonymous blog.
- Cisco's AR team runs a blog at blogs.cisco.com/ar/
- David Rossiter's blog is analystinsight.blogspot.com
- Hewlett-Packard's blog is at hp.com/blogs/analystrelations
- A blog by Hill & Knowlton's blog on analyst relations is available at blogs.hillandknowlton.com/blogs/Arcade.

**Communication Management Tools**

As long as a company's industry analyst relations program is managed by a single person, it may be sufficient to manage the communication with straightforward tools like an archive in the email system and MS Excel spreadsheets.

When more people need access to the data and when more people need to coordinate their communication, then such a simple approach is no longer sufficient. A common practice is to store information that is accessible for all involved individuals on a shared computer drive or on a special intranet website.

More sophisticated solutions are provided by companies like Augure or ARInsights.

Augure (*www.augure.com*) offers a communications management platform designed for agency and corporate use. It is not specifically designed for industry analyst relations, but with the needs of PR in mind. It may be a very useful tool if industry analyst relations is managed as an extension to a company's PR work only.

ARInsights (*www.arinsights.com*) has brought a very sophisticated tool to market called ARchitect™. The tool is tailored to the needs of industry analyst relations. It contains an analyst database, it allows to track all communication, it allows to coordinate across an industry analyst relations team that may be distributed across the globe and it allows for detailed reporting.

AR Intranet (analystrelations.webexone.com) contains productivity tools and information for industry analyst relations professionals. The provided information includes database directories of almost 4000 analysts, workflow tools and much more.

**Evaluation**

An industry analyst relations program can be evaluated in multiple ways (see respective chapter).

If an analyst program focuses on a small number of analysts only, then an evaluation may be very straightforward by analyzing the analysts' output, i.e. their research notes, their newsletters, etc.

Another approach may be the analysis of public quotes from industry analysts. This task can be done by media evaluation agencies like for example Echo Research (*www.echoresearch.com*) or others.

Finally, the Kensington Group – or KGI – (was based in Corte Madera, California) provided a very sophisticated annual evaluation of the effectiveness of corporation's industry analyst programs. It was founded in 1991 and ceased to exist end of 2005. Other companies like Lighthouse (*www.lighthousear.com*), SageCircle (*www.sagecircle.com*) and others are currently working on serving the Kensington Group's former clients. In this context it is interesting to note that the Kensington Group's former CEO Efrem Mallach joined Lighthouse in 2005 to lead the company's research activities.

A final resource we want to mention in this context is Tekrati (*www.tekrati.com*). Tekrati is based in the San Francisco Bay area. They do not only provide details about industry analysts (like profiles on *www.analystprofiles.com*), they also provide news on a daily basis on analysts, their firms and their research.

## Literature:


**WIN THEM OVER: A Survival Guide for Corporate Analyst/Consultant Relations Programs,** Efrem Mallach (First edition: 1987, second edition: 2007), ASIN: B000721JXS

**Crossing the Chasm,** Geoffrey A. Moore, HarperCollins, 1991, ISBN 0 8873 0519 9 (paperback: 0 8873 0717 5)

**Under The Influence,** article by Christopher Koch, Darwin (March 2001)

**Interview with Ed Gyurko**, article by K Srinivasan, PRPoint Newsletter (May 2002)

**Getting Results From Your Analyst Relations Strategies,** Louis Columbus, LWC Research – e-book available as PDF document (November 2004), ISBN: 0-595-33462-8

**Effective European Analyst Relations (Council Executive Breakfast),** Forrester Research, London (December 2005)

**The String Pullers,** article by Chris Kraeuter, Forbes (January 2006)

**ARmadgeddon** (online blog): *armadgeddon.blogspot.com*

**Analyst Equity** (online blog): *www.analystequity.com*

## About the Authors

**Dr Ralf Leinemann** has more than 18 years of experience working in international PR, marketing and business development departments in the high-tech industry. He holds a PhD in Physics from the University of Tübingen, Germany. He joined Hewlett-Packard in 1989, initially in technical marketing for real-time computer systems. Afterwards, Leinemann did product marketing for workstations and industrial systems. He then turned to business development for technical systems with a focus on the telecom industry, before he moved into Public Relations. He started his career in PR as the PR manager for HP's computing systems in EMEA (Europe, Middle East and Africa). He has done PR and industry analyst relations for a broad range of high tech products, both addressing business-to-business solutions as well as the consumer market. Today, Leinemann works for Matchcode, a globally operating marketing consulting firm providing end-to-end integrated marketing support from planning across execution to evaluation.

**Duncan Chapple** is an international authority on the development and evaluation of analyst relations teams within large multinational technology and telecoms companies. He has aided analyst relations professionals within over 80 companies including Avaya, BT, Cisco, Ericsson, Hewlett-Packard, Hitachi Data Systems, IBM, Siemens, Tata and T-Systems. Chapple has led Lighthouse Analyst Relations since 2002. Before Lighthouse he successfully founded and directed the international analyst relations business of Brodeur Worldwide. During the technology boom in the late 1990s Duncan was a consultant and analyst with Ovum, Europe's largest technology analyst house. Reflecting his prior background in high technology, Duncan is a Member of the British Computing Society, a Chartered Marketer and an advisory board member of Giersch Ventures GmbH. He played a central role in founding the Institute for Industry Analyst Relations, and was a member of its founding board.

Lightning Source UK Ltd.
Milton Keynes UK
UKOW05f0252190316

270488UK00012B/381/P

9 780906 378038